ZEN
AND
SHINTO

The Story of Japanese Philosophy

by

CHIKAO FUJISAWA, Ph. D.

GREENWOOD PRESS, PUBLISHERS
WESTPORT, CONNECTICUT

B
136
.F83
1971

The Library of Congress cataloged this book as follows:

Fujisawa, Chikao, 1893–
    Zen and Shinto; the story of Japanese philosophy. West-
port, Conn., Greenwood Press ₁1971, ᶜ1959₁

    92 p. 23 cm.

1. Philosophy, Japanese. 2. Zen Buddhism—Japan. 3. Shinto.
I. Title.

B136.F83 1971   181'.12   78–139133
ISBN 0–8371–5749–8   MARC

Library of Congress   71 ₁7₁

Copyright 1959 by Philosophical Library, Inc.

All rights reserved

Originally published in 1959 by Philosophical Library, New York

Reprinted with the permission of Philosophical Library, Inc.

Reprinted by Greenwood Press, Inc.

First Greenwood reprinting 1971
Second Greenwood reprinting 1974
Third Greenwood reprinting 1977

Library of Congress catalog card number 78-139133

ISBN 0-8371-5749-8

Printed in the United States of America

ZEN AND SHINTO
The Story of Japanese Philosophy

THE IMPACT OF SHINTOISM ON THE DEVELOPMENT OF JAPANESE ZEN

Having imbibed the fundamental messages of Taoism and Confucianism, both concerned with the exaltation of Tao, Mahayana Buddhism was brought over to Japan in 552 from China by way of Korea. It was the Prince Regent Shotoku Taishi (573-621), who left no stone unturned in attempting to assimilate all the phases of Buddhist metaphysics and arts. At the same time, he was versed in Confucian ethics and the political principles embodied in its basic teachings. Devout Buddhist that he was, the Prince never forgot to render respectful homage to the deities of Shinto indigenous to the Japanese soil, to whom the pedigree of the Imperial Family is thought to be traced back historically. In brief, he pursued assiduously his wise religious policies with a view to unfolding the spiritual potentialities latent in the Way of Kami. Therefore, what he accomplished by introducing Buddhism into Japan on a sweeping scale, was not to extirpate our national faith called Shinto, but to undertake to all intents and purposes

1

its conscious sublimation. The Roman Emperor Constantine ventured to overthrow the very foundations of ancestral folk-beliefs widely embraced by the Western people when he decided to convert to alien Christianism. Conversely, Shotoku Taishi betook himself to the arduous task of *Japanizing* Mahayana Buddhism by grafting it on the ever-growing stem of Shintoism. Therefore, the Prince is believed to have given expression to his firm convictions as follows:

Shinto is the root and stem and Confucianism the leaves and branches, while Buddhism is the flowers and fruits. Furthermore, he signalized Japan as the land specifically suitable for transplantation of the lofty principles of Mahayana Buddhism, because Shintoist universal relativism antecedently prepared the fertile and productive ground for the swift germination thereof. Our forefathers used to call our country by the name of "Sumera Mikuni," which carries the symbolic meaning: The Divine-Transparent-Clarity-Recuperative-Land. Otherwise stated, Japan is an all-integrative country restorative of existentialist clarity, whatever disruptive force may temporarily turn it into the confused state of turbidity. It is significant that our Emperor has unfailingly played this all-harmonizing and all-reconciling role by taking his wise and yet bold initiative in the digestion and assimilation of the substances of alien cultures. For this reason, he has been invariably held in religious veneration under the designation of "Sumera Mikoto": the Divine-Transparent-Clarity (Unity)-Recuperative-Prince. One has witnessed a most conspicuous exemplification of the clarifying and unifying function (displayed by the Japanese Emperor) in the accomplishment of the Meiji Imperial Restoration, when Emperor Meiji undertook an exterior modernization of the Japanese State encumbered with the clogging fetters of feudalistic customs. It was for the purpose of coping with the extreme precariousness of the international situation, which the Japanese people had to face willy-nilly at that moment. It is, however, vital to understand that the Great Sovereign proceeded to revitalize the Shinto faith before embarking on his gigantic plan to strengthen and solidify the basis of Japan in modern terms. As a result, Japan was able to steadily follow its progressive and innovating course of Westernization without running the risk of abandoning its distinct cultural individuality nurtured by the unscathed preservation of Shintoism. This phenomenological correlativeness of Sumera Mikoto and Sumera Mikuni exhibits the peculiar uniqueness of Shinto susceptible of tangibly combining objectivity and subjectivity into a dynamic whole. Therefrom arises the Shintoist principle concerning the identity of Land and Emperor.

This state of affairs finds its unequivocal expression in the interesting Shintoist concept of Kokutai or Kuni Gara: The Nation (State)-Body. The term

Gara or *Kara* has the existential connotation of ex or out of, as it presupposes something hidden and invisible appearing in the phenomenal world with no clear-cut distinction between transcendental unity and immanent diversity. In a word, "Kokutai" proves the magnifying in conception of the human body and a fresh approach to the study of Japanese culture from this psychosomatic point of view scarcely fails to yield a plentiful harvest which has never been thought of by the forerunners of Japanology who subscribed to the Western positivistic method setting aside any *subjective factor* as scientifically irrelevant and untenable. But we shall not understand what is meant by the inarticulate word "Kokutai" (the body of state), unless we grow well conversant with the purport of cosmic dialectics animating Japanese mythology which narrates how Japan was brought into being. *Kojiki* or the Records of Ancient Matters and *Nihon Shoki* or the Chronicle of Japan, which were respectively compiled in 712 A.D. and in 720 A.D. under the supervision of the Imperial Court, are held to be the authenticated works constitutive of a most reliable source for the study of Shintology. They furnish descriptions of myths, legends, folklore and historical accounts which throw much light on the basic relationships between the Imperial Family, the Japanese people, and the Land of Japan. Both open with a mythical story bearing on the essential aspects of Shinto cosmology. In particular, Kojiki relates

4

how the three Great Spirits (Kami) came into being on the High Plain of Heaven, when Heaven and Earth parted. They were named the Exalted-Heaven-Center-Lord-Deity (Ameno Minaka-mushi no Kami), the Exalted-High-Production-Deity (Takami Musubi no Kami), and the Divine-Production-Deity (Kami Musubi no Kami). They arose singly and then concealed themselves. The next Spirit which sprouted like a reed floating above the oily slime, was similar to a jelly fish. This deity was named the Princely-Spirit-of-the-Handsome-Reed (Umashi Ashikabizi no Kami).

In all, seven generations of Heavenly Deities succeeded each other in single splendour and at last the Male-Inviting-Deity (Izanagi no Mikoto) and the Female-Inviting-Deity (Izanami no Mikoto) appeared corporeally as the ancestors of all things. Thereupon, the Heavenly Deities commanded Izanagi and Izanami to procreate and consolidate the earth and gave them a celestial jewelled spear. So, the Divine Pair standing on the floating bridge of Heaven (presumably the rainbow) thrust down said spear into the brine and stirred with it until the brine began to curdle. When the spear was pulled up, some of the curdling dripped off and made a pile; finally, it became the island of Onokoro (the self-curdling).

The Divine Couple descended onto this island, where they built a Sacred Bower with a high thick pillar at its center. Around this pillar, the Female

Deity turned from the right to the left, while the Male Deity turned the same from the left to the right. When they met in this way, she first addressed herself to him: "Oh, what a fine and handsome youth you are!" Whereupon he courteously responded to her amorous call, saying: "How pretty and lovely a maiden you are!" When they thus became united in marriage, they begat a misshapen leech which they straightway placed in a reed-boat and sent adrift to the sea. Their next child was the foamy Island of Awaji, which they were reluctant to include in the number of their healthy and robust offspring. So, they had no choice but to go to Heaven for consultation with the Heavenly Gods. By means of divination, the latter found the true cause of their failure to be ascribable to woman's having spoken first, thus transgressing the Cosmic Law, for it gives precedence to the male, expansive, and positive principle over the female, contractive, and passive principle. Accordingly, the Divine Couple descended to their dwelling from heaven and turned round the Sacred Pillar again, this time the Male Deity going from the left and the female Deity from the right. When they met, he spoke first and said: "How charming and modest you are!" Then she answered blushingly: "You are really handsome and manly!" Thereafter, they gave birth to the main Eight Islands of Japan proper, together with a host of other smaller islands, the mountains, the valleys, the rivers, the trees, the grass,

6

the mists, and the winds. But, all these things pro-
created by the Divine Pair were overshadowed by the
appearance of the Heaven-Shining-Great-Deity or the
Sun Goddess, whose lineal descendants became successive Emperors of Japan. There are two versions
referring to the birth of the Sun Goddess. Nihon
Shoki reads in part: "We (Izanagi and Izanami) have
produced the Great-Eight-Island-Country with the
mountains, rivers, herbs and trees. Why should we
not produce someone who shall be lord of the Universe?" So, they gave birth to the Sun Goddess. But
Kojiki, considered the Bible of Shinto, relates in this
connection, that, when the Female Deity begat the
Spirit of the Fire, she was burnt to death and this sad
event plunged the Male Deity into the vortex of
sorrow and agony. He decided to go down to the
Nether World to solicit his wife to return to the
Sunny Land. In the meantime, he clandestinely
looked into the dark chamber where the putrefied
body of his dead spouse lay. Enraged at this insult,
she commanded the fiendish hags of Hell to seize
her treacherous husband. Taking to his heels, he
threw down a variety of articles he wore with a view
to halting his hideous pursuers. At last he succeeded
in reaching the Land of the Sunshine after having
blocked up the path through which the ugly females
were chasing him. On that occasion his first care was
to purify himself by bathing in the sea, as his sojourn
in the Dark Bottomland covered his body with stink-

ing filth. When he washed his left eye, the Sun Goddess sprang into existence. On washing his right eye and his nose, the Moon God and the Storm God were respectively produced. The Sun Goddess was instructed to reign supreme in Heaven as the Queen of the Universe, while the Night Realm was assigned to the Moon Deity. As regards the Tempest Deity, he was asked to rule over the oceanic waves and his ferociously wild nature seems to deify the typhoons which assail Japan in autumn. But, before departing, he ascended to Heaven in order to take leave of his sister (the Sun Goddess). He insulted her by breaking down the divisions made between her rice fields and by fouling the sacred hall where she celebrated the festival of first fruits. When he flayed a piebald colt and flung it into the room where she was weaving the garments of the deities, she lost all her patience with her brother's riotous acts and entered the Rock-Cave. Then, the world was plunged in utter darkness. The Eight Hundred Myriad Deities all in consternation held a divine conference at the Dry Bed of the Heavenly River (the Milky Way) with Omikane-no Mikoto, the wisest deity, presiding over its debates. First, all the singing birds were gathered so that they might prolong their cry for heralding the nearness of a dawn. Next, a huge sacred tree called Sakaki was uprooted from the Heavenly Mountain. They hung the beautiful string of Yasaka Jewels, the eight-sided mirror, and blue and white hemp offerings respectively on its upper, middle and lower branches. At this juncture, all the deities recited a divine liturgy (Norito) in chorus. A female deity called Ameno Uzume skillfully performed a mimic dance, while singing to the accompaniment of a sacred orchestra, from which Gagaku or the Ceremonial Court Music developed in later periods. Soon, the air resounded with the cheers and laughter of the Gods; the Sun Goddess unable to restrain her curiosity to learn the cause of this boisterous merriment peeped out of the cave and beheld her own radiant countenance reflected in the mirror. At this moment, the Hand-Strong-Deity rolled away a great stone which closed the entrance of the cave and pulled respectfully the Solar Goddess out of it. Thereafter, another deity surrounded the door of the heavenly grotto with a sacred straw rope called Shimenawa in Japanese. Several of the most important Shinto rituals and festivals owe their origin to this celestial event fraught with metaphysical significance. The collection of singing birds perched on gates facing the Heavenly Cavern led to the erection of "Torii" (literally meaning bird-rests) which we shall find in front of every Shinto shrine. When we visit the Shinto shrine, we unfailingly lay a twig of the Sakaki tree with evergreen leaves before its altar so as to enter into communion with Kami who is identical with the very source of cosmic vital energy. The mirror and the string of jewels form the Three Divine Treasures together with the sword which the Tempest God offered to the Sun Goddess. They are held to be the insignia of the Imperial Throne. Thus, in Japan, the ancient tradition stands cheek by jowl with modern progress. Finally, it came to pass that the Storm God was expelled from the High Plain of Heaven after heavy pains and penalties. Some time later, when the Sun Goddess commanded her grandchild called Ninigi no Mikoto to descend from heaven down to earth, she bestowed upon him the three sacred treasures referred to. Upon his descent, she blessed and glorified him by uttering the following words: "This Reed-Plain-1500-Autumn-Fair-Rice-Ear Land is the region of which my lineal descendants shall be lords. My august grandchild, do proceed thither and govern it. May prosperity attend thy dynasty, and may it endure forever like Heaven and Earth." About this time the Sun Goddess handed him the divine mirror and said as follows: "My grandchild, when thou lookest upon this mirror, let it be as if you wert looking on me. Let it be with thee on thy couch and in thy hall, and let it be a holy mirror to thee."

At present, this original mirror is found in the Inner Sanctuary (Naiku) of the Ise Grand Shrine. But, another mirror, which is its duplicate, is consecrated at the Awe-Inspiring-Place (Kashikodoko) located in the Tokyo Imperial Palace. This Rescript is usually called the First Divine Rescript of the Sun

10

Goddess. The marriage of the Crown Prince was celebrated on the tenth of April, 1959, in front of the Awe-Inspiring Palace and the Imperial Household solemnly reported this historical event to the Ise Grand Shrine.

The enduring continuity of our Shinto traditions which existentially concatenates the past and present finds no counterpart in any country of the world. There is Kamidana or the God Shelf within the Japanese dwelling, where one installs the undersized family shrine provided with a tiny mirror. It is before this domestic sanctuary that the head of the Japanese family is obligated to recite Shinto prayers called Narito (which means the enunciation of sacred words) day and night for the purpose of communing with the Sun Goddess who is ever venerated as the cosmic source of our life. The origin of the God Shelf is ascribed to a mythical legend, according to which the Male Deity Izanagi gave the Sun Goddess his sparkling necklace made of numerous precious gems, when she was born out of his left eye. Thereupon, she placed the sacred necklace (symbolic of the rice-ear laden with abundant grains) on a shelf of her storehouse, designating it as Mikura Dana no Kami or the Respectful-Store-House-Shelf-Deity. Against this Shintoist background, we can comprehend the reason why Zen Buddhism betokens the all-unifying operation of the Spiritually-Illumined-Mind as a mirror reverberating with all things without exception. What characterizes the Shinto-Weltanschauung is its mental preparedness to substantialize what has been speculatively expounded. Thus, the Buddhist teaching of "Suchness" became concretized as the Japanese way of thinking, prizing above all Naka-Ima (the Middle-Now) in which the verticality of time convergingly meets the horizontality of space.

The Second Divine Rescript the Sun Goddess conferred upon her grandchild refers to the delivery of the sacred rice indispensable for the feeding of the Japanese people. It reads as follows: "I will give over to my child the rice-ears of the sacred garden (Yuni-wa), of which I partake in the Plain of High Heaven (Takama go Hara)." This exceedingly important rescript is closely related to the story about the Food Goddess called Ukemochi no Kami. Once, the Sun Goddess asked the Moon God to see the Food Deity on her behalf. When he descended from heaven, she tendered him a hearty welcome. Then she turned her head toward the land, and forthwith from her mouth there came boiled rice; when she faced the sea, there came from the mouth things broad of fin and things narrow of fin. When she faced the mountains again there came from the mouth things rough of hair and things soft of hair. She placed these things upon one hundred tables for entertaining the heavenly messenger. But, the Moon God became flushed with anger, saying: "Do you dare feed me with nasty things disgorged from your mouth?" So, he drew his

12

sword, slew her, and returned to Heaven in order to inform the Sun Goddess of what had happened below. Upon hearing his report, she got exceedingly angry and said: "You are a wicked deity; I must not see you face to face." In this way, they became separated by one day and one night, dwelling apart. Some time after, the Sun Goddess sent again another messenger called Amekuma no Nushi to see the Food Deity. On the crown of her head there had been produced the ox and the horse; on the top of her forehead there had been produced millet; in her belly there had been produced rice; in her genitals there had been produced wheat, large beans, and small beans. He carried these things and delivered them to the Sun Goddess, who rejoiced, saying: "These are the very things, which the like-the-green-grass-ever-growing-human-race must eat and live by." So she made the millet, the panic, the wheat, and the beans, the seed for the dry fields, and the rice she made the seed for the water fields. It was very pleasant to look on the rice ears, eight span long, drooping to the ground in that fall. Moreover, she took the silkworms in her mouth and succeeded in reeling thread from them. Thus, she initiated the Japanese into the art of silkworm rearing. As the lineal descendant of the grandchild of the Sun Goddess, the Japanese Emperor makes it his duty to supply the people with an ample volume of rice necessary for the maintenance of their daily life. The Food Goddess

Ukemochi is worshipped at the Outer Sanctuary (Geku) in the Ise Grand Shrine and pilgrims are required to first pay homage to it, before they go to the Inner Sanctuary where the Sun Goddess is venerated.

In accordance with this time-honored tradition, the Emperor cultivates in person a model rice field located within the Imperial Palace in order to constantly keep in memory what is solemnly enunciated in the Second Divine Rescript issued by the August Imperial Ancestress. For the same reason the Empress is engaged in the rearing of silkworms in her own chamber. It is in pursuance of this tradition that immediately after the termination of the war, Emperor Hirohito paid a visit to General MacArthur with a view to requesting the latter to deliver sufficient food to the Japanese people exposed to the peril of starvation. At the same time, he is believed to have told the Supreme Commander of the Allied Forces that he would willingly go to the gallows assuming full and complete responsibility for the calamitous defeat. This absolutely egoless attitude of his apparently motivated General MacArthur to respect the Imperial Household. In consequence, the General strenuously resisted the Soviet plan by which the Communists wanted to abolish the Japanese dynasty, taking advantage of the post-bellum social conditions. In fact, the serene, simple and sincere mentality of Sumera Mikoto is the virtual realization

14

of what Zen Buddhism understands by entrance into Nirvana. Whereas the powerful military governments organized by the Heike, the Genji, the Toyotomi, the Ashikaga, the Tokugawa, and the Tojo have crumbled one after another, the Japanese Imperial Dynasty has lasted and will last perpetually, being coeval with Heaven and Earth. So, I wish to call the Imperial Rule *Sumeracracy*, because of its being fundamentally different from *Monarchy* as developed in the West, which is substantially the same as the Tokugawa Shogunate. Bearing this historical fact in mind, one will readily understand why the overwhelming majority of the Japanese are dissatisfied with the present Constitution, which stipulates in Article I that the Emperor derives his position from the will of the people, with whom resides sovereignty. Anyone conversant with the all-unifying idiosyncrasy of "Sumera Mikoto," to whom all the Japanese will feel impelled to existentially submit themselves as "Mikoto," will take notice of the great blunder the Occupation Authorities have made in imposing the present constitution on the Japanese nation. There are many reasons to believe that General MacArthur entertained the very unfortunate idea to supplant Shinto by Christianity on the plea of the latter being incomparably superior to the former, viewed from a religious point of view. But, I am afraid that this universally unjustifiable preconception only reveals the imperviousness of some Western religious think-

15

ers to the fundamental postulates of *depth psychology,* which scientifically approaches the dimensional depths of the psyche for the purpose of recuperating the dynamic unity of faith and reason. Candor compels me to avow that faith and reason are not well soldered in dogmatism adhered to by the established Christian Churches irrespective of whether they be Catholic or Protestant. But, in Shinto, there is no gulf between faith and reason because it has never lost its primal contact with the sustaining dimension of the depths of life, from which all special beliefs must have emerged in the past. Therefrom derives the proverbial tolerance of Shinto, which willingly admits co-existence with other faiths.

In reference to what should be believed in as a future global faith of all mankind, Arthur Koestler writes that religion has become sealed off from contact with logical reasoning. The incompatibility between the two halves of the split mind was smoothed over by the churches' diplomatic appeasement of science and by the believers' psychological resistance against admitting this split. Nevertheless, the sad fact remains that, in the West, religion is widely dealt with as a *spiritual luxury.* Man looks forward to receiving a new, spontaneous type of faith capable of restoring the *navel cord,* through which he receives the saps of cosmic awareness without reducing him to mental infancy. This sort of *psychical faith* should provide ethical guidance, teach the lost art of con-

16

templation, and restore contact with the supernatural without demanding reason to abdicate. We Neo-Shintoists are persuaded that a new scientific reappraisal of Shintoism will lead to the laying of a cornerstone of such a planetary simple faith capable of keeping pace with the incessant advancement of depth psychology. Shinto is a tangible living reality and the compact body of the Japanese people numbering approximately 100 million and possessing a racial and cultural *homogeneity* without parallel are theoretically "the Shintoists," although most of them are not conscious of this extremely important fact.

The Third Divine Rescript demonstrative of the essential nature of Shinto or the Way of Kami was given by the High-Production-Deity (Takami Musubi no Kami) appearing together with the Sun Goddess. This Deity is also called the High-Tree-Deity (Taka ki no Kami), inasmuch as he is evidently the sanctification of cosmic vital energy enshrined in "the Tree of Life." In this connection it must be recollected that upon his descent from heaven, the grandchild of the Sun Goddess was accompanied by the Five Attendant Deities: Ameno Koyane no Mikoto (the first ancestor of the Nakatomi priest family), Futo Dama no Mikoto (the first ancestor of the Imbe priest family), Ameno Uzume no Mikoto (the first ancestor of the Sarume dancer family), Ishikori Dome no Mikoto (the first ancestor of the Mirror-Makers), and Tamaya no Mikoto (the first ancestor of the Jewel-Makers).

It must be noted that the High-Tree-Deity issued the Third Divine Rescript specifically for *the two divine princes* preoccupied with the observance of Shinto rituals as intermediary between Emperor and people. It reads:

> "I will set up a sacred tree of life imbued with the solar energy (Himorogi) and a sacred enclosure (Iwasaka) to perform ritualistic ceremonies for the sake of my descendants (Sumera Mikoto). Do, ye, Ameno Koyane no Mikoto and Futo Dama no Mikoto, take with you also Himorogi, and go down to the Central Land of Reed-Plains (Japan). Moreover, ye will there perform ritualistic ceremonies in favor of my Imperial descendants."

It must be recalled that deities played a momentous role by deracinating a large Sakaki tree, and reciting Shinto liturgies, when the eighty myriads Kami racked their brains how to entice the Sun Goddess out of the heavenly cave. Besides, their offspring turned out to be the principal priest families specializing in the performance of Shinto rites designed to phenomenologically connect Sumera Mikoto and the Japanese people. The name of the posterity of Ameno Koyane no Mikoto is "O Naka Tomi," meaning the Great-Middle-Subjective serving as a sort of

18

medium between the heavenly deities and the Emperor on one hand and as religious mediator between the Emperor and the people on the other. The key word "Hi" has many a meaning: the Sun, the number one, spirit, soul, ice, scarlet, water-pipe, life, and so on. Therefore, *Shinto semantics* can help us to decipher such enigmatically ambiguous terms as were used in ancient Shintology.

In Japanese, man is called "Hito," which carries the metaphysical connotation of the *sun's temporary-tarrying-place*, because he owes his individual existence biologically to cosmic vitality stored within the Sun. Hime, equivalent to princess in English, is a combination of the Sun (Hi) and woman (Me). What C. G. Jung calls "individuation" which means the unfolding and integration of human individuality, will prove helpful to the grasp of the Japanese idea of "Hito." According to the interpretation of Dr. Ira Progoff, *individuation* encompasses all the varied stages and phases of development, by which the human organism emerges as a personality.

In a word, the meta-psychical interrelation of Emperor (as the lineal descendant of the Sun Goddess) and people is not different from that of the Sun and myriads of sunbeams. But for the Sun there would be no irradiation of solar rays. It is precisely on this ground that we Neo-Shintoists categorically demand the revision of the present Constitution, for it is guided by the strange idea that sunbeams can generate the Sun. Conspicuously enough, those who advocate this un-Shintoistic Constitution betray a complete absence of understanding for depth psychology owing to their rationalistic minds thinking along mechanical lines.

It is important to realize that Himorogi and Iwasaka are the prototype of the Japanese Shinto shrine called Yashiro or Jinja in Japanese. The Shinto shrine consists of Haiden or hall of worship and Keidai or the enclosure abounding in a variety of holy trees which correspond respectively to Himorogi and Iwasaka. From the thatched roof of the hall of worship soar skywards crossbeams in the form of an X and this vertical projection, reminiscent of the Heavenly Pillar, must be looked upon as a kind of "spiritual antenna," enabling man to come into existential communication with Kami.

The wooden architecture of the Ise Grand Shrine is the purest expression of the original and genuine taste peculiar to the Japanese people, who are fond of simplicity, purity, spontaneity, brightness and sincerity. It is rebuilt every twenty years faithfully preserving its original structure.

In following the Third Divine Rescript, the Japanese people will visit the Shinto shrine to offer fervent prayers to the Heavenly Deities for the attainment of longevity and prosperity of the Emperor. In response to them, the Heavenly Deities represented by the Sacred-High-Tree-God will also pray for the

20

health and happiness of the Emperor. Thus, both Heaven (Kami) and Earth (Man) concur in attempting to strengthen the life and body of Sumera Mikoto incarnating the Eternal Now (Naka Ima), since his dynasty has never suffered interruption from time immemorial down to the present. Despite its disastrous consequences, the defeat has not affected *the everlastingness* of the Imperial Throne. There is no denying that Zen Buddhists see in this historical reality of Japan a concrete expression of the absolute present or the absolute here-now.

From the foregoing it can be gathered that the Japanese refrain from praying for the enjoyment of their individual prosperity and happiness by making pilgrimages to the Shinto shrine. It is axiomatic that Shinto is "Communal Faith," while Buddhism or Christianism are "Individual Faiths." Hence it follows that the Japanese can be both Shintoists and Buddhists, or Christians without involving any contradiction because of the dimensional difference of their respective qualifications. On New Year's day hundreds of thousands of Japanese throng to the Meiji Shrine dedicated to the cult of Emperor Meiji, regardless of whether they be Buddhists or Christians. That the Shinto shrine has evolved out of Himorogi, namely "The Sacred Tree comprising the solar productive power," will serve to articulate the implications of the Way of the Tree of Life, of which mention is made in *Genesis* in the Hebrew Bible:

21

"the Lord God placed at the East of the Garden of Eden Cherubim and a flaming sword, which turns in every direction in order to protect the Way of the Tree of Life."

We Neo-Shintoists believe that the Way of the Tree of Life is to be identified with Shintoism or the Way of Kami because the latter treats the deity and the wooden pillar (Hashira) as identical. In other words, the Path of the Tree of Life has been preserved intact in Japan under the designation of Shinto. The Westerners considering themselves to be descendants of Adam and Eve, who ate the fruits of "The Tree of Knowledge" in transgression of the Divine Command, have become inextricably bound up in the dualistic view of life which contrasts religious spirituality with scientific materiality. They seem to be groping in the dark in quest of a new global orientation of life capable of restoring their mental equilibrium and stability.

I am convinced that they can be cured from this fatal malady of schizophrenia by plucking the refreshing fruits of the metaphysical Tree of Life hitherto concealed in Japan. It is somewhat sarcastic that the Anti-Shinto Directives which were enacted by the Occupation Authorities allow us to undertake with freedom scientific clarification of our Shinto faith, national and yet universal in significance and application. Anyhow, universalization of Shinto will make a considerable contribution to the emergence of a new type of global psychic faith which can keep our brain from splitting into the two halves. It is not until all attempts at a spiritual revival within the framework of the established churches become widely recognized as a futile abortion that a great and simple *dynamic religion* will come to the fore.

The esoteric meta-technique, by virtue of which the Emperor will be enabled to enjoy his longevity and health, is named the Soul-Tranquilizing-Rite (Mitama Shizume, Chinkon Sai). The Shinto priests officiating at the Imperial Court (supposedly descendants of Ameno Koyane no Mikoto and Futo Dama no Mikoto) perform this very important ritual by beseeching the Eight-Musubi-Deities domiciled in the Himoro (the Japanese Tree of Life) to cooperate with them for accomplishing the meta-psychic technique in question. In brief, it aims to coordinate and reintegrate all the dismembered selfs into One Cosmic Major Self. It is interesting that this grand ritual characteristic of Shintoism is doubtlessly the same process as *Yoga*, which is a specific method for reaching longevity by harmoniously regulating the exhaling and inhaling movements of breath. Both "Yoga" and "Musubi" mean union or connection allusive to the possibility of recuperating all-unifying cosmic consciousness, to which modern man has become oblivious, floundering as he does in the morass of sheer materialism. The solemn ceremony of Mitema Shizume instituted for preserving the robust health of Sumera Mikoto consists in the fastening of the Sacred Thread ten times.

It is said that the purpose of the soul-pacifying ritual is to bring the wandering soul of the Emperor back into the middle part of his body. In this respect, a great deal of resemblance can be noticed between Mitama Shizume and the physical posture of "sitting-meditation" (zazen) assumed by the Zen monk. Seated on padded cushions with his legs crossed, he regulates his respiration so as to outbreathe from the belly (Hara in Japanese), rather than from the chest. This will shift the body's center of gravity to the abdomen, while the slow and easy breathing from the belly fosters the meditative mood conducive to spiritual clarity.

The perpetual operation of Tao is plainly emblematized by the Three Sacred Treasures, the mirror, the sword, and the necklace of comma-shaped jewels. We can visualize the unifying, potentializing power of the mirror, the diversifying, actualizing power of the sword, and the coordinating, interconnecting power of the necklace of curved jewels by observing carefully the growth of the Sacred Tree of Life. The seed sprouts into a tiny seedling which, in turn, sprouts sideways a number of twigs; it is not long before a big tree impregnated with the cosmic vital sap comes into existence. This expansive movement of *digression* culminates in efflorescence of beautiful blossoms (the sword). Then, the contractive movement of *convergence* will set in, with the result that the flowers, by shrinking, metamorphose into the fruits in which multiple seeds will be found (the mirror).

It is, however, owing to the interlinking power of Tao (Michi in Japanese) that the perpetual cycle of seed-production carries on (the necklace of curved jewels) with uninterruptedness. It is perhaps for this reason that our forefathers used to hang on the upper, middle, and lower branches of the Sakaki Sacred Tree, the mirror, the jewels, and the sword, respectively.

In ancient China, Tao was often portrayed with the chart of Taiichi (Taikyoku in Japanese). This esoteric diagram shows that it contains in embryo the dual forces of yin (black) and yang (white). The ideographs Tai and Chi respectively signify "greater than great" and "the cosmic life symbolized by the tree developed by the collaboration of heaven, earth, and man, who makes use of the mouth (the language) and the hand (the action) for this purpose." A black dot (the germ of yin) within the white semi-circle will gradually develop into the black semi-circle, whereas a white dot (the germ of yang) will follow the reverse course by causing yin to give place, step by step, to the growing movement of yang.

A serpentine line linking the white and black semi-circumferences is suggestive of the process of pulsatory alternation incessantly going on in the universe.

25

The two perceptible potencies of yin and yang polarize out of the matrix of the imperceptible fountainhead of Taiichi. Chu Shi, the founder of Neo-Confucianism of the Sung Dynasty, wrote a famous essay with the object of explaining the all-harmonizing function of Taiichi which is to be identified with Tao in the final analysis.

He called Taiichi (Taikyoku in Japanese) the Great Ultimate or the Great Void. The Great Ultimate in motion generates yang or the active and bright principle; at rest, it generates yin or the passive and dark principle. This alternation repeats itself eternally, motion tending to rest, and rest passing over again into motion.

The male and female principles produce all things without exception. The *Book of Changes* explains the productive power wielded by Taiichi as follows: "There is the Cause of all things called Taiichi. It generates the Two Primary Forces called Yin and Yang. Yin and Yang generate the Four Images corresponding to Spring, Summer, Autumn and Winter. The Four Images generate the Eight Trigrams." So it may be concluded that this extremely intriguing theory of Taiichi expounds in abstract terms what is concretely visualized in the Shinto Third Divine Rescript relating to the Sacred Tree or Himorogi. It is evident that the Christmas Tree and the pine and bamboo branches erected in front of the entrance of the Japanese dwelling house on New Year's day are

26

both variants of Himorogi.

Shinto means the Way (Tao in Chinese) of Kami, deifying the cosmic vitality generative of all beings, animate and inanimate. We understand by the Way a *permanent center* of the Universe to be apprehended intuitively within incessant mutations. Kami is taken to mean the productive power of Taiichi. Therefrom springs the fundamental theory of Oriental political science, in accordance with which unity is discernible beneath diversity and the many and the one are inseparably interwoven with each other. It is important to understand that our Sumeracracy (Japanese Monarchy) is exactly patterned after the Way or Tao, because its aspect of immutable permanency (unity) is represented by the continual Line of Imperial Dynasty unbroken for ages eternal, while successive emperors (Sumera Mikoto) who were born and passed away unceasingly represent its aspect of perpetual mutation (diversity).

Sumera Mikoto signifying the Divine Prince capable of restoring the original oneness of things proves the personalized unifying center of the Japanese nation. It is he who is in a position to harmonize the centrifugal force of *individualization* and the centripetal force of *co-ordination* with each other, the Japanese key word Sumera meaning dynamic unification or all-settling transparency. Through his constant performance of Shinto rituals (Matsuri), he will prevent *self-consciousness* from encroaching upon the proper domain of *sub-consciousness* operative in the depth of our mind. On the other hand, the Japanese who are called *Mikoto* will never fail to turn to *Sumera Mikoto* for their spiritual guidance in case of emergency and it is for this reason that Matsuri must be fully understood not as a private affair of the Imperial Family, but as an exceedingly momentous act to be executed for the benefit of the whole nation. We believe firmly that revitalization of ancient pure Shinto purged of its spurious and external paraphernalia can make a tremendous contribution toward the easing of the strains and stresses attendant upon the Cold War. Prior to explaining the primordial substance of Shinto, at once national and universal in outlook, we wish to request Western nations to make a clean sweep of their preconception that religious monotheism based on the principle of *abstract universality* alone is entitled to being adhered to by civilized people, whereas any polytheistic or pantheistic faith as believed in by most of Asian and African nations cannot be held in esteem on account of its primitivity.

C. G. Jung, who has accomplished a remarkable spadework in re-appraising ancient myths, brings out the close correlation to be found between the conscious direct thinking clearly expressed in modern science and techniques and the unconscious fantasy thinking which once activated the minds of our primitive forefathers. He vehemently combats the wrong sociological view that remote primitiveness is tantamount to *ignorant barbarity* which will be repudiated by the progress of scientific civilization. Indeed, it will be an unwarranted presumption to imagine that we are more energetic or more intelligent than were the ancient people of the remote past. We have become certainly rich in objective knowledge but very poor in matured wisdom as preeminently revealed in mythology. The modern man pours nearly all his creative power into the sole object of consummating his material knowledge, while the ancient man devoted his whole energy to the mythical contemplation of the living Cosmos. So, the activity of the early classical mind, artistic in the highest degree, showed indifference to the modern way of thinking, striving to understand the real world as objectively and accurately as possible.

According to C. G. Jung, it is through fantasy thinking that modern rationalistic thought can be brought into contact with the subconscious layers of the human mind long buried beneath the threshold of consciousness. It is, however, undeniable that the devitalizing process of technological civilization impels modern intellectuals to turn again to mythical truth for psychic guidance. Being viewed from this angle, Shinto, in deifying the generative force of Nature as the Sun Goddess, will never fail to attract them, inasmuch as they became disillusioned by the abstract sterility of so-called world religion, which is fighting desperately against fearful odds—Marxist Communism which holds actually one third of the world's population in its tight grip.

The time has finally come for the Neo-Shintoists to embark on "universalization" of the Way of Kami for the sake of harmonizing the divergent claims of the Democrats and Communists, both estranged from Cosmic Truth as ingrained in ancient Shinto pure and simple.

The Christian theology teaches us that God created man out of the dust of the earth and breathed into his nostrils the breath of life. As a result, there is no direct line of connection between *Divine Transcendence* and *Human Immanence* and it is apparently from this theological dogma that Western dualist philosophy stems, which opposes the spirit to the flesh and sets God against Satan.

The Cold War is evidently a modern version of the perpetual strife between Christ and Antichrist.

In contradistinction to the Western traditional theology, the Japanese Shintoist theology identifies the original relationship of Kami (God) and man with that of parent and child. In other terms, Kami begat man, instead of having created him, as is mentioned in the Holy Bible. On the one hand, Kami as parent and man as child are considered different entities; but, on the other, they cannot be separated from each other because of their sharing one and the same divine blood. So, to borrow the theological terminology of the West, heavenly transcendence and earthly immanence interpenetrate each other, while spiritual untangibility becomes one with biological tangibility. It is thanks to the unceasing flow of the Divine Blood in circulation that *ancient tradition* is brought into concordance with *modern progress*. The Way of Kami or Shinto is called "Kami nagara no Michi" in pure Japanese: The out-of-the-divine-spirit-spontaneously-welling-forth-sacred-blood.

For this reason, all the Japanese people venerate the Sun Goddess as the cosmic source of their respective lives, and they install in their dwellings a miniature domestic shrine, within which a sacred symbol of the Sun Goddess is consecrated and in front of which they clap their hands day and night in attempting to commune spiritually with her. In this connection, it will be necessary to dwell on the fact that Japanese should, without exception, be devout followers of Shinto conceived of as *communal faith;* at the same time, they may be believers in either Christianity or Buddhism, both falling within the purview of *individual faith.*

In accordance with the mythical book called Kojiki or the Records of Ancient Matters, the Male Deity Izanagi and the Female Deity Izanami united in marriage gave birth to all beings animate and inanimate. Hence, it follows that man, the land, the mountain, the river, the valley, mist, the tree, grass and other things partake of the identical status of

"Hara Kara" or the out-of-the-womb-of-the-Divine-Mother-born brethren. Therefrom sprang the Japanese political theory, which establishes the identity between Sumera Mikoto, the All-Unifying-Divine-Prince (Emperor) revered as lineal descendent of the Sun Goddess, and Sumera Mikuni, the All-Unifying-Divine-Land (Japan). This Shinto view of life will be grasped articulately by studying some key-words such as Mono and Utsuwa. Mono signifies both man and thing, whereas Utsuwa means both a personal ability and a material vessel. A unique feature of Shinto resides in its combining harmoniously Buddhist *pantheism* which urges every individual to meditate in order to reach spiritual enlightenment, denying a transcendental God, and Christian *monotheism* which makes absolute faith in God contingent on salvation, precluding any chance of attainment to heavenly bliss through individual effort. In short, Shinto can be re-christened as *"pantheistic monotheism,"* since its monotheistic aspect is revealed unifyingly in Ameno-Minakanushi-ne-Kami or the Heaven-Middle-Lord-Deity, while its pantheistic aspect is revealed diversifyingly in a myriad of deities.

Pursuant to Shinto vitalistic dialectics, the ultimate source of cosmic life deified as the Heaven-Middle-Lord-Deity polarizes alternately into the male, expansive, and differentiating potency and the female, contractive, and re-integrating potency which are respectively deified as Takami Musubi no

32

Kami or the soaring-up-productive-Deity and Kami Musubi no Kami or the divine-productive-Deity. It is through the rejoining of these diverging and converging forces relatively opposed to each other, that a new life will be continually produced. For instance, the tree can bear fruit owing to the alternating succession of the waxing seasons of Spring and Summer, and the waning seasons of Autumn and Winter. One designates this natural law perpetually at work in the Universe as *Musubi*. This important word signifies "the germinative sun" and "the action of binding" as well, for combination of the swelling male agency and the absorbing female agency can germinate anything whatsoever. It is due to the full operation of this rounding-out cosmic principle of Musubi that Japan was able to blend harmoniously the immaterial cultures of East as exemplified in Buddhism, Confucianism, and Taoism, and the material civilization of the West based on science and technics. In the same fashion, Japan can reconcile perfectly American capitalism, which emphasizes only too unilaterally *political freedom* and Soviet communism, which stresses only too unilaterally *economic equality*, into a new pattern of Musubi-economy which renders the unobstructed display of individual creative impulses compatible with the appropriate regulation of production for meeting the requirements of a community as a whole. Under these circumstances, Japan should refrain from siding

33

politically either with the U.S.A. or with the Soviet Union, holding fast to her supreme position transcending all conflicts and divergencies. It is incumbent upon the Japanese people to do their utmost to convince the leaders of both ideological camps of the absolute necessity of relinquishing their armaments race, prejudicial to the advent of enduring world peace.

As a preliminary step towards the effectuation of this global project permeated with the harmonizing spirit of Shinto, we Neo-Shintoists have set up the Shinto International Academy for the promotion of *planetary consciousness,* while fostering frequent personal contacts between ideologically conflicting parties. To speak more concretely, Japanese Neo-Shintoists should take the initiative of dissuading the Capitalist democrats and Marxist totalitarians from pursuing their pernicious *"power politics,"* by creating a congenial and persuasive atmosphere among them. The cogency of our arguments drawing upon Shinto Musubi-vitalistic-dialectics lies in our being able to offer the means of removing the fatal divergence between individualistic American democracy and communistic Russian dictatorship. It is precisely due to the lack of a *middle connecting link* that the individualizing tendency of capitalism comes into frontal clash with the socializing tendency of communism; this glaring contradiction must be averred as the upshot of the Western theology which opposes a transcendental God to immanent man. The disconnecting of religious spirituality from scientific materiality characterizing Western civilization was brought forth historically in consequence of the extirpation of the ancient folk faiths indigenous to Greek, Roman, and Germanic peoples. The lamentable extinction of "the Western way of Kami," supposedly the same as Shinto in substance, has led to the obliteration of what might be termed *"the cosmic vitalizing continuum"* (The Sacred Blood or Michi), which can bring about the fusion of transcendental unity and immanent diversity. The Way can be envisaged as the permanent center intuitively grasped amidst incessant mutations, now showing the diversifying tendency, now showing the unifying tendency.

Therefrom derives unequivocally *the occidental philosophy of dualism,* which pits theistic Vatican fiercely against atheistic Kremlin. This naked fact gives evidence that Western thought is rapidly forfeiting its universal validity which has once commanded the respect of humanity regardless of East or West.

It can hardly be doubted that *the specious philosophy of existence* propounded by some agonizing thinkers in Western Europe must be looked upon as a desperate attempt to reunite immanence and transcendence in one way or another. Confronted with such a trend of novel thought looming large on the world's mental horizon, we must endeavor to diffuse universally the fundamental teachings of Shinto, so as to meet the yearnings of humanity standing on the verge of a tremendous catastrophe. While, in the West, Christianity, introduced from without, severed irretrievably the actualities of present-day life from the traditions of remote antiquity, in Japan Shinto digested and assimilated the cream of cream of Buddhism to be compared with Christianity in the profundity of abstract spirituality.

Consequently, Japan has been exercising a *dynamic power* capable of simplifying all things complex and complicated and it is in this synthetical harmony that the visible and the invisible, and the metaphysical and physical remain undivided. This is related to the core of Japanese *aesthetic symbolism* to which a great many foreigners will feel irresistibly attracted. *There are four different stages in the evolution of Western Christianity.* The first stage covered the period of contact with Greek civilization and it was Thomas Aquinas who created the system of Christian theology by rationalizing the faith of Jesus by means of Aristotelian philosophy. The second period was covered by ancient Rome, which organized the Catholic Church and elaborated the ecclesiastical laws. The third period was characterized by the encounter of Roman Catholicism with the individualistic Germanic peoples who challenged the overweening religious authority. As a result, Protestantism raised its claim of individual salvation in defiance of the Roman religious hierarchy. The fourth period brought Christianity into touch with the English and American pragmatic thinking, while the latter introduced the concept of social salvation centered around welfare work.

The writer of this book wishes to add a fifth period, conjured up by an impetuous onslaught of atheist Marxism against the Christian religion, while branding it as an opiate misused for hypnotizing the ignorant masses of the people. Western Christianism being incompatible with Soviet atheism, Japanese Neo-Shintoists reason that survival of Christianity depends upon its confluence with Shinto which blends idealism and materialism into an archetype of *meta-realism* acceptable to both ideological groups.

To sum up the above statements, the incompatibility of *abstract universality* and *concrete nationality* in the Western way of thinking is traced back to the Christian theology, which posits the unnatural alienation of transcendental omnipotent God from immanent enslaved man, *groaning under the lugubrious burden of original sin.*

But, we shall be able to eliminate this fatal antinomy by formulating a new concept of *concrete diversified universality* on the basis of Shinto, according to which all nations partake of a divine nature, as they were born out of the matrix of one and the same Sun Goddess. It is in Japan that the Way of the Tree of Life as mentioned in *Genesis* of the Holy

Bible is jealously guarded against desecration on the part of Adam and Eve, who came to discern the difference between good and evil by having eaten the forbidden fruit of the Tree of Knowledge. *The Sacred Tree of Life is the prototype of the Shinto shrine surrounded by a holy forest.* The Tree of Life is called *Himorogi,* or the tree containing in its bosom the solar energy which comes into full play, thanks to the operation of Musubi dialectics. It is to be noted in this connection that Shinto can be defined anew as "pantheistic monotheism," for it can harmonize Christian heavenly monotheism and Buddhist earthly pantheism through the intermediary of the Tree of Life, whose root sinks deep into the ground and whose crown towers high toward the sky.

In the light of *Shinto cosmic vitalism,* we comprehend that objectivity and subjectivity are, as it were, organically correlated in ultimate reality, all-comprehensive and all-reconciling. What amounts to ultimate reality is called Makoto in our language. Makoto carries, however, the three different connotations: the true word, the true thing or truth, and sincerity. So, this key word helps us to apprehend that only utmost sincerity can open the massive portal of Divine Truth, remaining hidden to modern rationalized man, because he clings stubbornly to his blind faith in so-called "scientific objectivism."

But, in recent decades, those Western philosophers who insist upon the primacy of existence try to clarify what purports to be "the subjectivity of truth," for any abstract universality must be regarded merely as an illusion concocted by formal logic incapable of seizing concrete reality. Martin Heidegger and Gabriel Marcel, two prominent representatives of Western Existentialism, concur in demanding that the *abstract conceptual verity be transformed into the concrete inwardness of a vivid spiritual experience.*

Dr. J. B. Rhine, proponent of the new science of *para-psychology,* which deals with extra-sensory perceptions such as telepathy, clairvoyance, clairaudience, and premonition, argues that the clash of ideologies in the contemporary disintegrated world has arisen primarily from disagreement in the interpretation of the basic nature of "man." He points out the fact that a great majority of intellectuals reject *dogmatic revelationistic religion,* since it is unable to counter the claims and promises of Marxist communism.

Any dogmatic and speculative religion which lures us into the evanescent world beyond must be taken as a vain, misguided and enslaving fiction. Therefore, we cannot but recognize a certain portion of truth being comprised in the blunt assertion of materialistic ideology actuating the Soviet Union. As Dr. Rhine says, parapsychology will elucidate some day all the *psi* implications of human global personality, thereby supplanting both the materialistic philosophy of communism and the decaying structures of the old religious organizations which the Marxists themselves have been successfully replacing.

In a word, the transscientific and transreligious laws of nature will finally emerge triumphantly from the chaotically disoriented world of the present day to account coherently for the existence of an orderly spiritual reality, which lies beyond the reach of Marxist ideology. To speak with candor, we hope that exasperating proselytism will cease to sow the seeds of religious discord among the so-called heathenish peoples intent upon a conscious revival of their earth-near ancestral faiths.

The time has come at last to reassess Shinto cosmic dynamics as the very forerunner of Western existentialist philosophy which is as yet groping its way toward ultimate reality: our racial forefathers happened to spotlight with intuitive immediacy the objective and subjective interrelatedness of Cosmic Truth. They also created an esoteric system of *Japanese semantics* designated as Kototama no Manabi, the word-soul-doctrine which lays hold of all-compelling truth by probing deeply into our mother tongue, at once physical and metaphysical in structure. As Ernst Cassirer rightfully maintained, *language and myth must be taken as twin creatures of prehistoric origin*. In fact, we can train ourselves to get hold of mythical traces of times gone by, by conducting intensive philological researches. This is particularly true with regard to the study of the

40

ancient history of Japan which reaches back into unfathomable antiquity. By probing into Japanese mythology, we are struck by the fact that *Mikoto* means concurrently deity, the sacred word, and life.

In this connection, it is of vital importance to understand that *all theoretical cognition* takes its departure from a world already "preformed" by language. So, any person desiring to create a logical system of rationalistic philosophy must draw *its building stones* from the quarry of words which cannot be dealt with in theoretical terms.

We Neo-Shintoists wish to construe Shinto afresh as a dialectical synthesis enabling the male, diversifying, and dilating force (consciousness) and the female, unifying, and absorbing force (unconsciousness) to blend harmoniously, so that a new life can be unceasingly generated. According to this Shintoist way of thinking, capitalistic liberalism which prevails in America proves to be but a manifestation of the expansive and individualizing potency of the Way (Michi or the Sacred Blood) which is identical with catholic truth, while Marxist socialism raised to the guiding principle in Russia proves to be but a manifestation of the contractive and totalizing potency of the same. The reason why they are opposed irreconcilably to each other is that they have fallen away from the absolute Way, from which they were originally polarized.

It is noteworthy that no other country but Japan

preserves the Way of Kami intact, which corresponds to the Way of the Tree of Life. D. C. Holtom, an American clergyman, who showed a great deal of understanding for the intrinsic value of Shinto, wrote in his illuminating work *Modern Japan and Shinto Nationalism* something like this. The communal folk religions which the ancestors of Western peoples once wholeheartedly and unreflectingly espoused are gone forever as a living system of ritual and belief; their sacred world presided over by ancient tribal Gods was broken by their subsequent conversion to alien Christianity, whose uncompromising and at the same time universalizing monotheism dissolved the inner bonds with their racial forebears; the old communal form of religion, which was normal in the West two thousand years ago, still exists in Japan today as a powerful religious force capable of merging the individual destiny with the greater destiny of the nation. By enlarging on this salient feature of Shinto philosophy, the national destiny of Japan can be inseparably linked with the universal destiny of all mankind. Accordingly, this Shinto *planetary theory* will urge all nations to participate in the building of a global human community based on the exalting idea of brotherly solidarity. We Neo-Shintoists feel called upon to do our best to induce the other nations to reintegrate themselves spontaneously and voluntarily into one single human family. Far from contenting our-

42

selves with merely criticizing the ideological defects inherent in both individualistic democracy and totalitarian communism, we are anxious to show them the tangible and concrete way, whereby they can attain to Cosmic Truth palpably revealed in Shinto. Now that both the U.S.A. and the Soviet Union are cautious so as to avoid the risk of provoking annihilating nuclear war, Japan should avail herself of this golden opportunity to take *the psychical offensive* for the outlawry of all war.

George F. Kennan, former American Ambassador to Russia, is reported to have said that the communist danger is not a military threat, nothing in Marxist doctrine supporting the spread of world communism by armed force. In any case, it will be unwise for the U.S.A. to try to subdue its sullen arch-enemy with overwhelming military power. In casting a glance at the present day world nobody will gainsay that Japan is fully qualified to act as impartial ideological arbiter for the two blocs which are misconstruing a half-truth to be full truth.

As aforementioned, if Japan keeps from allying herself militarily either with the U.S.A. or with the Soviet Union in carrying out her planetary policy for the total defense of the earth itself, all other nations will esteem her courageous and constructive leaders who are ever ready to render unconditional service to humanity without *arrière-pensée*. It is a foregone conclusion that the true and genuine teachings of *Shinto realistic Catholicism* will be willingly accepted by both American democrats and Russian communists, because they will be compelled to admit the compatibility of free individualism and controlled communism and of religious idealism and scientific materialism in the light of Shinto.

Now that fourteen years have elapsed since the end of the war, we shall have to get consciously rid of the shameful plight of mental lethargy and psychic paralysis into which the appalling defeat had plunged our nation with devastating consequences. We note indignantly that our academic and journalistic leaders are unreasonably disdainful of our time-hallowed culture, being *grovelingly subservient* to alien political ideologies which are hardly consistent with the basic teachings derived from our lofty Shinto cosmic view of life. Symbolically Shinto can be compared to a sparkling diamond not yet fully polished, whereas its facets represent so many ideologies, such as idealism, realism, democracy, Marxism and the like. Thus one will be able to catch hold of the cosmic wholeness of the Way of Kami by putting these partial ideas into brackets, so to speak. This inwardly compressed psychical process is designated in Japanese as *Sumera* or the clarification of all the impurities in a coordinating pellucidity and it is Sumera Mikoto who is obligated to fulfill this all-reconciling function with the strict observance of *Chikonsai* or the Soul-pacification-ritualistic-ceremony, an esoteric meta-technique

44

(similar to Yoga), capable of re-integrating the split mental state into a dynamic harmony.

This is the reason why the Japanese people will entreat Sumera Mikoto to vouchsafe them guidance, in case they are spiritually stalemated beyond hope. What characterizes his consummate personality purged of all shades of egotism is a subtle combination of "inner sageship" and outer statesmanship. Of the three sacred treasures symbolical of the Japanese Imperial Throne, *the Divine Mirror* worshipped at the Ise Grand Shrine as well as at the Awe-Inspiring-Place erected within the Imperial Palace in Tokyo and *the Divine Sword* consecrated at Atsuta located in the vicinity of Nagoya refer respectively to sageship and statesmanship to be cultivated by the Emperor. It is evident that the Divine Mirror emblematizes the unifying spiritual power of *religion* and the Divine Sword the diversifying analytical power of *science*. But, as to the *Divine Necklace of Curved Jewels*, it is denotative of the interlocking of religious unity and scientific variety. It is noteworthy in this regard that the remote antiquity can be brought into unison with the modern age, thanks to the intermediate agency of the Divine Curved Jewels suggestive of the uninterrupted continuity of our historical tradition. In Western countries, the ancient and modern times are in conflict with each other, because the interconnecting factor, as is indicated in the Third Divine Treasure, is absent.

To reiterate what was said about the Divine Mirror, we shall be prompted to conduct a serious introspection by looking into its polished surface on which our countenance is faithfully reflected. We call the mirror *Kagami* in Japanese, which implies alike the condensation of *Kami* and *Kami* to stoop or to bend forward (Kagamu), an allusion to the accomplishment of spiritual self-contraction.

So, we Neo-Shintoists are convinced that a *sweeping renovation* of Shinto, which constitutes the permanent backbone and mainstay of Japan, can alone overcome the impending crisis with which we are confronted. This consideration has prompted us to create the above-mentioned Shinto International Academy in order to meet the pressing requirements of the times. It is, above all, designed to conduct objective and disinterested studies in the fundamentals of Shinto using accurate scientific methods. This Academy must, therefore, be regarded as an *intellectual clearing house* called upon to facilitate free exchange of views and opinions bearing on mutual understanding of Orient and Occident. Furthermore, its staff members are in readiness to provide foreign students of Japan with the essential knowledge about Shinto and other kindred subjects, such a Buddhism, Taoism, and Confucianism. It is gratifying that UNESCO has carefully elaborated a major project with a view to accelerating *mutual appreciation* of Eastern and Western cultural values. It was put into effect at the begin-

ning of 1957 for as long a period as ten years. Its saga-
cious drafters admonish particularly Western nations
to strive to achieve a better understanding of the
characteristic traits of Oriental traditions, because the
latter have not as yet been explored sufficiently from
a scientific point of view. Evidently, a warped and
preconceived judgment can often bring about more
misunderstandings than *total ignorance,* especially
when assessing divergent moral and religious values
not sufficiently elucidated theretofore. This subject
assumes all the greater seriousness as, in our time,
no religion is allowed to impose itself upon another,
much less destroy it. So, it must be taken for granted
that no nation is entitled to forcibly convert other
people to the religion it embraces. A growing awareness of the equality of the nations in the exercise of
full freedom to unfold the spiritual and cultural
potentialities of their own should be given due consideration when seeking to foster mutual comprehension of East and West. According to the philosophy
of UNESCO which underlies its multiple activities,
the current idea that *material superiority* and *tem-
poral power* necessarily denote a "superior civiliza-
ion" must be energetically refuted, since wounded
susceptibilities resulting therefrom will lead inevita-
bly to utter spiritual estrangement between East and
West. As a matter of fact, endeavors must be made to
throw off complexes which Oriental people have
acquired on occasion owing to their having been

brought under the tutelage of great Western powers for many centuries. *UNESCO stands for reconciliation of regard for national cultural particularities with universalist aims.* This basic orientation of thought is in full consonance with the Shintoist view of life which enables us to harmonize perfectly the one and the many into *concrete universality.*

Under these circumstances, we are obligated to take exception to those flaccid *progressive men of culture* (Shimpoteki Bunka Jin in Japanese) who are frowning suspiciously upon a spontaneous resurgence of the Shinto belief which is not to be uprooted from the deepest layer of our racial consciousness. In our eagerness to throw into relief the pristine core of Shinto, we decided to adopt for all to note the following slogans: "No Japan without Shinto" and "The existentialist indivisibility of Sumera-Mikuni and Sumera-Mikoto." We shall also proceed to mobilize a number of scholars and thinkers possessed of mental flexibility and resiliency requisite to apprehend immediately the grave situation. Our intellectuals should have mustered their moral courage to protest intrepidly against the unjustifiable condemnation of Shinto even at the risk of their lives. Therein lies obviously a fatal flaw of our national character expressing itself conspicuously in unconditional submission to any superior political power. Hence, exaltation of the democratic spirit after the war served the purpose of removing a great deal of this our

48

weakness by stimulating a keen sense of individual freedom and responsibility which had been developed but little in this country. But, this does not mean that the Western type of individualistic democracy fits Japan in its entirety, since our Sumeracracy basically transcends the conflict between autocracy and democracy so characteristic of the modern West. In a word, one must renew Sumeracracy as a meta-democracy.

We believe that a sincere and fructifying dialogue carried on between the elite of different nations will pave the way for ultimate realization of durable global peace. Consequently, we wish to claim candidly *full rehabilitation of the honor and integrity* of Shinto, which came to suffer preposterous distortion and ignominious perversion during the period of the Occupation. In other words, the Anti-Shinto Directive enacted by the Supreme Commander of the Allied Forces forbade all the educational institutions of this country to use any teacher's manual or text book which makes mention of any Shinto doctrine. It prohibited likewise the educational authorities from making pilgrimages to Shinto sanctuaries inclusive of the Ise Grand Shrine dedicated to the Sun Goddess, not to speak of the taboo put on our participation in Shinto rituals or ceremonies associated with the Japanese State. At that time, the Ministry of Education had to issue instructions under duress to all Japanese school teachers to the effect that the anti-Shintoist idea contained in said Directive should be implemented to the detriment of the full preservation of our national faith.

It was due to the success of this *psychological warfare* that our post-bellum youth turned into miserable thought-vagrants uprooted from the solid ground of our millenary tradition. But, an overwhelming majority of the Japanese are hesitating to give vent to their pent-up resentment in regard to this challenging act of outrage against Shinto, because of their introvertively reticent and reserved idiosyncrasy. We Neo-Shintoists are, however, grimly determined to nullify the present-day Occupation Constitution, permeated as it is with the corrosive spirit of the Anti-Shinto Directive against the cosmic hierarchy perennially maintained between Tenno and people. We are not so much concerned with the question as to whether Article IX relating to *disarmament* should be revised, but with the complete repudiation of the false conception that the Emperor must derive his position from the general will of the people with whom resides sole sovereignty. It is conceivable that some of our war-time military and bureaucratic leaders have misintepreted Shinto to be a militarist ideology, for they were incorrigibly trained in the Western political way of thinking which dualistically contrasts monarchical autocracy with popular democracy. But, we must again corroborate all-harmonizing pure Shinto, purely and simply, as the most tolerant and peaceful meta-religious faith imaginable, distinguishing it from rigidly monotheistic Western religion. Under the all-reconciling and all-unifying influence of Shinto, the Japanese people have succeeded in digesting and assimilating Eastern and Western cultures without losing their cultural individuality. Besides, it is to be noted that no religious war has occurred in Japan, thanks to the proverbially conciliatory attitude which our Shintoist faith has so far taken towards anything whatsoever. In a word, sensible people in this country go so far as to contend that the harsh censure and ruthless expulsion of Shinto by the Occupation Authorities should be regarded as an aggressive deed of *spiritual imperialism* likely to hamper the achievement of deep mutual understanding between Japan and America. Legally speaking, the Anti-Shinto Directive issued on December 15, 1945, ceased to be valid with the formal declaration of independence of Japan. But the recalcitrant offspring it has spawned are still alive, running amuck almost with impunity. They are the MacArthur Constitution which deliberately inverted the pre-reflexive relation between Sumera Mikoto (Tenno) and Mikoto (people), the Imperial Rescript on the Renunciation of the Emperor's Divinity so insidiously imposed on the war-prostrate government; the enactment of the juridical foundation law relative to religion by which meta-religious Shinto was made degradingly identical with any ordinary religion; the exclusion of Japanese history and geography, organically concatenated with our Shinto traditions, from school curricula; the emergence of the General Federation of Labor Unions (Sonyo) and the Teachers Union of Japan (Nikkyoso) bent on the frustration of unity and stability in industry and education; the negation of the grand principle relevant to the unity of Shinto ritual and government through rendering *Matsuri* merely a private matter of the Imperial Family; the abolition of the Imperial Rescript on Education promulgated in October, 1890, by Emperor Meiji, etc. Let us quote:

"Know Ye, Our Subjects:

Our Imperial Ancestors have founded Our Empire on a basis broad and everlasting, and have deeply and firmly implanted virtue; our subjects ever united in loyalty and filial piety have from generation to generation illustrated the beauty thereof. This is the glory of the fundamental character of Our Empire, and herein also lies the source of Our education. Ye, our subjects, be filial to your parents, affectionate to your brothers and sisters; as husbands and wives be harmonious, as friends true; bear yourselves in modesty and moderation; extend your benevolence to all; pursue learning and cultivate arts, and thereby develop intellectual faculties and perfect moral powers; furthermore, advance public good and promote common interests; always respect the Constitution and observe the laws; should emergency arise, offer yourselves courageously to the State; and thus guard and maintain the prosperity of our Imperial Throne coeval with heaven and earth. So shall ye be not only Our good and faithful subjects but render illustrious the best tradition of your forefathers.

The Way here set forth is indeed the teaching bequeathed by our Imperial Ancestors, to be observed alike by Their Descendants (Successive Emperors) and the subjects, *infallible in all ages and true in all places.* It is Our wish to lay it to heart in all reverence, in *common with you,* Our subjects, *that we may attain to the same virtue.* The 30th day of the 10th month of the 23rd year of Meiji."

A careful perusal of this historical document will convince anybody that the noble principle of moral collaboration governing the basic relationship of Emperor and people is synonymous with the Cosmic Way (Michi) which perpetually operates in great nature, while transcending the narrow confines of time and space. So, the *body politic* (Kokutai) of Japanese Sumeracracy pertains neither to despotic monarchy nor popular democracy which came to the fore in revolt against the extravagances of the former.

In Japan, Sumeracracy can rise above the low dimension of antinomy between monarchy and democracy as set at variance in the West and this is unequivocally owing to the Shintoist theology being repugnant to separate what is above from below. As Sumera Mikoto the Emperor is under obligation to follow the politico-moral teachings left by his Imperial Forefathers with unswerving fidelity. *Sumeracratic statecraft* will never run the risk of degenerating into tyrannical misrule. The lamentable fact remains, however, that the militarist and bureaucratic caste often ventured to intervene between the Emperor and the people with the sinister design of usurping the Imperial Prerogatives for the effectuation of their political ambitions. In this respect, the defeat has served to dispel the dark clouds which thwarted the sunshine to penetrate into the yearning hearts of the masses of our people.

Let us quote a significant passage out of Holtom's work entitled *Modern Japan and Shinto Nationalism*:

"There were three bonds between the throne and the people that were chiefly exploited by the ruling oligarchy. They were sacredness, benevolence, and power or authority. The three were so tightly interwoven by skilful governmental fingers that the manifestation of one was the manifestation of all. *Sacredness* was a means to power through religious qualifications; *benevo-*

lence was a way to the same end through moral qualifications; *authority,* that is, *power* exercised by virtue of legal, moral and religious capacities, was the goal of all."

Although we are not in full agreement with this view, its biting criticism gives us much food for deep meditation. In fact, we felt relieved from the stifling atmosphere of official regimentation, when the pre-war autocratic government became stripped of its power to suppress any sort of sound criticism liable to undermine its absurd authoritarianism. Despite our grim determination to nullify the substance of the Anti-Shinto Directive, we are honest and frank enough to avow that our people have scandalously neglected to delve deep into the cosmic truth hidden in the recesses of Shinto. Our perfunctory attitude has emboldened our ruling oligarchy (mentally modelled after the Western dualistic way of thinking) to pervert at will Shinto philosophy.

So, the aim of said Directive to prevent recurrence of the perversion of Shinto theory and beliefs into militaristic and ultra-nationalistic propaganda designed to delude the Japanese people and lead them into wars of aggression must be given due consideration, as a means of purifying original Shinto from its subsequent adjuncts, which vitiate its genuineness. To summarize the foregoing statement, our government should clearly enunciate, at home and abroad, that the Anti-Shinto Directive has been already invalidated and that the anomalies created by its forcible application in the realms of politics, economy, and education must be resolutely liquidated, whatever objections the so-called "defeat parvenu" (who benefited undeservedly by the Anti-Shinto Policies of the Occupation Authorities) may be tempted to raise against our legitimate claim.

There is no denying the fact that the great majority of the highly mediocre politicians who ran the Meiji bureaucratic Government were senior graduates from the law department of the Tokyo Imperial University. They were primarily initiated into the dualistic thought-orientation prevalent in the modern West, while they were prone to look down upon the Japanese idea which excels in intuitive cognition as backward and out of date. When Emperor Meiji sent his court chamberlain to the Tokyo Imperial University in 1887, in order to inquire whether there were some professors specializing in Oriental metaphysics, President Watanabe bluntly retorted that Asia has never produced any system of philosophy worthy of the name. So, it was natural that students of said university preoccupied with the wholesale introduction of Western learning should have identified our Sumeracracy indiscriminately with monarchical autocracy in the Occident, which clashed irreconcilably with popular democracy over political supremacy. In their opinion any political principle contrary to monarchy was considered provocative of a violent revolution bound to undermine its foundation. In other words, they became so indoctrinated with Western dualism that they were unable to distinguish Western monarchy inimical to democratic liberalism from Japanese Sumeracracy which revolves around the affectionate parent-child relationship between Emperor and people. Let us remind ourselves that a famous controversy which arose over the Meiji Constitution between the authoritarian Professor Uesugi and the Liberalist Professor Minobe far from clarified the existential attributes of Sumera Mikoto functioning as the highest Shinto medium-priest. Therefore, we would like to exhort our intelligentsia to liberate themselves from the fetters of Western dualist thinking in order that they may take cognizance of concrete universality revealed in Shinto meta-scientific vitalism. We know for certain that the new trend in world ideas will culminate in a harmonization of subjective idealism and objective materialism which have thus far been opposed to each other. This sudden convulsion of human thought demonstrates that Shinto is becoming gradually universalized under the names of phenomenology or existentialism.

It is essential to note that the prelogical framework of Sumera Mikuni (the Japanese family-state) is the same as the structure of the atom, around whose nucleus a certain number of electrons swiftly move in their regular orbit. In brief, what amounts to the nucleus of the Japanese state is Sumera Mikoto, towards whom the Japanese people will gravitate intuitively.

Master Reiju Tsubaki, founder of the Great Truth Association established at Hakodate, Hokkaido, struck a novel note by bringing forth a body of esoteric teachings alike meta-religious and meta-scientific in conception. According to his religious philosophy, *our physical body is a living holy Bible,* because any psychic movement happening within ourselves will give rise to a vibrational wave in our flesh without fail. But, what is more important is that a painful vibration caused by hatred will destroy our body before long and this dreadful experience can be forestalled if timely measures can be applied against the perpetration of an atrocious crime.

In the mirror of transcendental science propounded by Master Tsubaki, the political leaders of the great Western powers who embarked upon the inhuman tests of A and H bombs cannot escape their fate of perishing sooner or later amidst the murmurs of pathetic complaints and wailing grievances. Furthermore, Master Tsubaki says that the intensification of our idea-wave can change the psyche of others so completely, that we need no physical compulsion for bringing our enemy to his knees. In fact, a small-scale popular campaign launched by a few housewives in Japan with a view to suspension of H bomb tests has swelled into a universal movement and eventually it happened that the Government of the U.S.A. announced the cessation of nuclear tests for one year. The meta-scientific lore created by Master Tsubaki is to be averred as a conscious renewal of pure ancient Shinto.

As J. W. T. Mason, an American enthusiastic student of Shinto pointed out in his outstanding treatise on Shinto entitled *The Meaning of Shinto* (published in 1935 by E. P. Dutton & Co., Inc., New York), Japan is now faced with the urgent necessity of bringing the intuitive knowledge of reality inherent in Shinto to the surface of the modern mind which craves scientific articulation. In fact, the modern age of intellectual development calls for presentation of any knowledge in terms of self-conscious comprehension as well as intuitive implication. Otherwise, Shinto will go the same way as other primeval intuitive truths which became finally extinct. So, we Neo-Shintoists insist upon a thoroughgoing revival of Shinto along the lines of self-consciousness, self-expression, and analytical originality. It is expedient Shinto which reconciles scientific practicality and religious spirituality by virtue of its all-unifying aestheticism.

The essential feature of Shinto lies in its vital surge capable of expanding transcendence into immanence. For Shintoists, the universe is the self-development of the Divine Spirit or Kami. The Shinto mythology will be able to restore the primeval truth of life, while keeping to the basic idea of modern progress, as a fresh inspiration for germinative action. In brief, the material originates in the immaterial, to follow the fundamental tenets of Shinto *metaphysical realism.* Shinto is our communal faith calculated to co-ordinate harmoniously all individual faiths such as Buddhism and Christianism. One will admit that, in other countries than Japan, there once existed what purports to be the very counterpart of Shinto, prior to the advent of any abstract world religion. In view of the cleavage being increasingly deepened between *Christian theism* and *Marxist atheism,* the thinking people the world over appear to be nostalgic for the cradle of their primordial life, in which the spiritual and material are undivided.

One will discover in Shinto a communal vitalistic faith, enabling us to enter into direct communion with the very fountainhead of cosmic life, ever throbbing rhythmically in the universe. When all the nations feel spontaneously urged to revert to this very source of their respective lives ascertained to be Shinto, there will be gradually realized a *psychical unity of mankind.* As a result, Shinto will be universalized to meet the exigencies of the times. In fact, the Japanese people can make great contributions to world civilization, when they learn how to explain the fundamental characteristics of their Shinto culture and train themselves in the advantages of analytical methodology. As long as we remain mentally restrained and do not develop self-consciousness, we will not be able to play the momentous part in the world to which our creative capacities entitle us.

The Japanese people can become aware of the noble spirit of their own culture only by comprehending Shinto in modern ways of self-expression.

One will never grasp Shinto by continuing to remain subordinated to Chinese intellectualism. Hindu philosophy, and Western materialism. Japan has superiority over the West in intuitive feeling and subconscious understanding of life; in Shinto, Japan has a conception of universal creative spirit, which is more realistic than the spirituality of the West. But, under modern conditions, self-expression and analytical efficiency are more necessary to develop human welfare than is inner feeling. If Japan is able to retain her intuitive and subconscious powers and at the same time develop self-consciousness and scientific ability, Japanese culture will be carried to heights not yet reached by any other nation. But the spirit of Japan and the creative conception of Shinto will fall into a subconscious morass and become more ineffective in aiding Japan's future progress, if the Japanese mind continues to look beyond Japan for mental orientation, instead of unfolding the originality of self-consciousness within the nation itself.

In spite of Shinto being intrinsically "transcendental realism" of the highest order, the way in which it has been approached heretofore is anything but satisfactory, since Western people who go by the empirical theory of *modern progress* have been swayed by the obstinate bias that *primitiveness* is precisely the antithesis of *civilization* which is their pride.

Viewed from this narrow position, Shinto may be belittled as the vestige of an ancient folk belief, which is destined to fade into insignificance, in proportion as monotheistic world religion makes headway. But, disappointing any sanguine anticipation by the sophisticated intelligentsia, the invisible pendulum of the cosmic movement is beginning to swing abruptly from the divergent lines of "progress" towards the convergent ones of "regress."

As a result, the Orient which lay dormant is being thrust again into the foreground in keeping with the alternating rhythm of the way (Tao), which corresponds to what the Westerners usually call "perennial philosophy."

Withdrawal of the troops of England and France —with the backing of the U.S.A.—from the Suez Canal zone and the spontaneous occurrence of the Anti-Soviet revolution in Hungary have come to impress us that any Western imperialist power can no longer quell the vitalistic upsurge of *existentialist nationalism,* heralding the forthcoming advent of a transmodern age.

The contemporary Americans who enjoy a highly efficient technological civilization are eccentrically crazy with the jazz music which originated in primitive Africa.

This bizarre phenomenon is a plain attestation of their *mechanized* minds who pine anew for re-union with the very source of their vital energies.

The Western philosophy of existence which aims at the vitalization of *reason* as well as the rationalization of *life* is undoubtedly an unmistakable revelation of the Cosmic Way of a Europe obsessed by the specter of another conflagration. Martin Heidegger, a pioneering representative of German existentialist philosophy, sees the grave of truth in objective certainty and rationalizing knowledge which account for man's alienation from Being (*das Sein*) as substantially identical with Japanese Kami. It is vital to remark that what he designates as "the essential thought" (*das Seinsdenken*) involves a radical reversal of the modern shallow mode of thinking which opposes the subject to the object.

Thus, essential thought precedes not only the distinction between subjectivity and objectivity, but also the division of thought itself into the theoretical and practical. It enables us to encounter hidden Being and to participate in its inscrutable transcendental secrets. The unifying direction of transcendence is the vertical one towards Being as against the ramifying direction of immanence, which is the horizontal one perceivable in the world of science and technics. Being is at once the *thrower* (from the one to the many) and the *caller* (from the many to the one).

So, human existence is a projection from the hidden depth of "transcendental reality" which we cannot gauge experimentally and positivistically.

According to Heidegger, Being remains an invaluable treasure buried in this devitalized world which is subordinated to the prosaic technological order. The homelessness or self-alienation of modern man left to the mercy of all-denying *nihilism* cannot be overcome otherwise than by his recuperating "genuine selfhood" rooted in what Heidegger defines as *meta-physical nothingness* susceptible of effacing the antinomy between the subjective and objective. To be sure quantity and causality are concepts incorrectly transferred from the *physical* to the *psychical*, intuition being the only possible way to penetrate into spiritual reality.

We Neo-Shintoists hold human existence to be pre-reflectively constitutive of, and connatural with, transcendence and immanence, for man is called upon to form a metaphysical trinity together with heaven and earth.

What the Western existentialists generally criticize as human alienation is estrangement of man not only from heavenly spirituality but also from earthly materiality. So, they will wrestle with the extravagances of speculative idealism because of its denaturing man and the world, while they will vehemently confute the excessively unilateral theories advanced by sheer materialism, such as the Marxist ideology.

In short, their primary concern is with finding man's correct place which is to be inextricably inserted in the nexus of heaven and earth. Heidegger appreciates the Marxian theory of human alienation (occasioned by exploiting capitalism) as the most realistic grasp of the fate of man historically conditioned and actually embedded in material circumstances. But, the technical outlook of Marxism which countenances further conquest of nature is extremely critical, as it is far from removing the root-cause of "human self-estrangement." Presumably on account of his imperviousness to the spontaneous outflow of filial piety, Karl Marx overlooked the important fact that man's labor can produce no goods without taciturn *concurrence of mother nature.* The efficient productivity of labor would be inconceivable but for the delivery by nature of a voluminous quantity of fuels such as coal and oil.

It is a foregone conclusion that Marxism, which imputes all social evils objectively to the defective economic system of capitalism and remains subjectively indifferent to the metaphysical problem of radicalizing the modern ego-centered and over-subjective attitude, will be swept away by the mounting tidal wave of *cosmic vitalism* unceasingly at work in our Shinto tradition.

The existentialist philosophy, which has emerged as a reaction of the philosophy of integral *man* against the excesses of the philosophy of *ideas* as well as the philosophy of *things,* will discover its purest possible archetype in the Way of Kami to be identified with the Path of the Tree of Life.

The Japanese myth narrates that the Sun Goddess—deification of the procreative force of nature—commanded her grandson to descend from heaven to earth, so that he might combine transcendence and immanence and that his lineal descendants become succesive Emperors of Japan charged with the holy duty of sublimating the unauthentic existence into the authentic one through constant performance of Shinto rites. In fact, Sumera Mikoto is the very point of confluence of transcendental Being and immanent world.

It must be pointed out in this respect that Heidegger is believed to have expounded the sun *metaphysically* as Being *(das Sein),* because his concept of authenticated man *(das Dasein)* is the same as the Shintoist one of "Hito" which is *the spot wherein the sun tarries for a certain length of time.* It is more than a haphazard conjecture that Heidegger is under the impetus of unquenchable desire to push his metapsychic thought as far back as the remotest antiquity when the pagan Germans observed the cult of the sun along with its corollary of ancestor worship. We wish to liken individual existence to a multitude of sunbeams which will be absorbed into the solar orb upon their leaving this world. It is significant that heaven to which the departed soul ascends, is called in Japanese Hi-no-Waka-Miya, or the rejuvenescent solar palace. So much for the comparative study of Heidegger's ontology and Japanese Shintology.

Now, let us refer to a striking affinity which we can find between Shinto and the metaphysics of Gabriel Marcel who visited Japan last fall to give a series of lectures at a number of our universities. The uniqueness of his original philosophy resides in the contrast of the primary intellectual reflection with the secondary intuitive reflection. Whilst the primary reflection works horizontally, analytically, and destructively in the world of objects, the secondary reflection works vertically, integrally, and constructively in the realm of innermost personal experience. We exercise the former abstractly and conceptually, whereas we exercise the latter concretely and vitally in order to restore the unity of living and thinking. Marcel felt irresistibly attracted towards what Shinto esoterically stands for, when he was cordially received in audience by Sumera Mikoto. Pursuant to Shintology, the primary reflection and the secondary one correspond respectively to the expansive male activity displayed by Tamami-Musubi-no-Kami and the contractive female activity displayed by Kami-Musubi-no-Kami.

To recapitulate what we explained above, both Heidegger and Marcel are to be considered *theoretical exponents* of Shintoist meta-science, although they are as yet unconscious of the role they are playing.

By going over once more what I have stated above, it will be realized that *Zen Buddhism,* introduced from China by the Japanese monk Eisai (1141-1215), who established Zen monasteries in Kyoto and Kamakura, found a most fertile soil in Japan for its fullest possible development, because Shinto was capable of concretely vitalizing the basic teachings of Zennism abstractively expounded in China. Hence, it is against the historical background of Shintoism that the salient features of Japanese Zennism, excelling in practical simplicity and cognitive straightforwardness, can be fully understood. It is, however, unfortunate that this important problem has not been given due consideration in view of Shintology's lagging behind on account of the lack of a method adequate to its scientific clarification.

THE ESSENTIAL CHARACTERISTICS OF
ZEN BUDDHISM

A grasp of Zen Buddhism will pave the way for a thoroughgoing comprehension of Japanese traditional culture envisaged as a whole. In effect, the fine and subtle spirit of Zen pervades all walks of our national life, while it has made a tremendous contribution toward the development of literature, art, manners, ceremonies and dancing, in Japan. So, it is quite natural that intelligent Westerners should find in Zennism the very key to the unlocking of the main portal of Japanese civilization. But, few people are aware of the undeniable fact that Zen Buddhism was able to reach the culminating point of its development under the overwhelming influence of Shintoism, which constitutes permanently the kernel of the Japanese existential thought-pattern.

Had it not been for the interaction and interpenetration of Shinto and Buddhism, we would not have produced what amounts to our global culture, as it stands today. It is precisely for this reason that a penetrating scrutiny must be undertaken to point out the close interrelatedness and the pronounced interplay of Zen Buddhistic and Shintoistic cosmic phenomenology, whose concrete universality must be approached from a meta-religious as well as a meta-scientific point of view. For all his erudition, wisdom, and acumen, Dr. Taisetsu Suzuki has so far failed to bring to light this basic subject matter so fundamental to a clarification of the outstanding features of Japanese history and tradition. It would not be an exaggeration to contend that the lack of keen insight into the very core of Shinto will preclude the likelihood of probing into the parapsychological profundity of our culture which is unique in its kind. An attempt to render justice to the merits of Shinto in all fairness is all the more imperative, as this national faith of ours has become grossly misunderstood on the part of most of the Western intelligentsia bedeviled by the theological dogmatism which is prone to dualistically contrast transcendentality with immanency.

It is true that the Anti-Shinto Directives the Occupation Authorities issued on December 15th, 1945, have induced us to conduct a deep reflection upon the way in which bigoted and narrow-minded Shintoists used to misinterpret Shintoism in prewar times, as if it were a hotbed of militarist ideology. But, the stunning defeat Japan suffered has come to purge the old anachronistic Shinto of its spurious externals, so as to readjust its essential teachings appropriately to the existentialist requirements of the times. The hap-

70

py matrimonial union of the Crown Prince and a commoner's daughter performed in accordance with the Shinto ritualistic tradition, gave impetus to a fresh reappraisal and conscious vitalization of Shinto world conception. On this auspicious occasion we Neo-Shintoists were determined to do our best to recuperate the mental autonomy as well as the psychic stability of the Japanese people who have been thrust into the sad plight of political confusion and spiritual disintegration.

Before trying to spotlight the interrelation detectable between Zen Buddhism and Shinto, it will be necessary to make a brief statement with respect to the characteristics of Zen Buddhism. It is taken for granted that Zen has grown out of a subtle merger of Indian Buddhism with Chinese Taoism, whose founder Lao Tze is believed to have been an older contemporary of Confucius. Buddhism initiated by Gautama the Buddha (born about 560 B.C.) emphasizes the absolute necessity of realizing one's salvation through attainment of *spiritul awakening* in this world. This means that one will be released from suffering by entering into Nirvana with spontaneity.

The sublime idea of Nirvana is in contrast with the Christian Gospel of salvation to be achieved through absolute faith in the Savior and demonstration of this faith by the performance of supernatural miracles. We are accustomed to classify Buddhism into two groups respectively designated as Hinayana

Buddhism or the teaching of the Lesser Vehicle and Mahayana Buddhism or the teaching of the Greater Vehicle. We understand that the vehicle is a spiritual carriage which can conduct us to the other shore.

Hinayana Buddhism primarily preoccupies itself with realization of the passive world-shunning ideal entertained by Arhat (Rakan in Japanese). An Arhat is a monk who wishes to renounce the secular world along with his family responsibilities and duties in order to enter individualistically into Nirvana. But, Mahayana Buddhism centered in the elucidation of the doctrine of the Void. Nothingness as well as the Middle Way aim at consummation of what the Bodhisattva idealistically stands for. As a potential Buddha, the Bodhisattva refrains from withdrawing from this world replete with suffering, qualms, treachery and mistrust, because he deems it his ordained mission to enlighten himself and others alike through the fulfillment of his religious activities, which go hand in hand with the exercise of political wisdom. In other words, he desires to postpone his blissful entrance into Nirvana from his deep and genuine feeling of compassion which prompts him to devote his individual life to the salvation of all others by riding in common on the Grand Vehicle. He strives to extend his vivid experience of sudden spiritual awakening to those who are as yet covered over with pitch dark *ignorance* or Mumyo, signifying the total absence of spiritual clarity. In this respect, Mahayana

72

Buddhism seems to have been indelibly influenced by the Confucian political philosophy which links "inner sageship" with "outer statesmanship." In this connection mention must be made of Maitreya, who will appear 5000 years after the death of Gautama as a new Buddha with a view to saving this defiled world immersed in the ocean of unrighteousness and perversion. Obviously, the Bodhisattva is called upon to play this messianic role which devolves upon Maitreya who is all kindness and compassion.

Buddha set forth the Four Noble Truths, by virtue of which we shall be able to arrive at the ultimate goal of our spiritual journey ending with the entrance into Nirvana.

The First Noble Truth teaches us that human existence is reduced to suffering, because it is miserably subjected to an endless succession of sufferings occasioned by impermanence, transiency, and uncertainty inherent in all things. Thus, human existence unavoidably involves birth, sickness, sorrow, grief, decay, precariousness, dotage and death. Our life is illusory, evanescent, and unhappy with no prospect of depriving the process of its mutability and decomposition.

The Second Noble Truth teaches us that all suffering owes its inception to selfish craving. We try to fulfill our unquenchable desire by exploiting both other human beings and the surrounding world as a means to satisfy our own self-centered ends.

The Third Noble Truth teaches us that all suffering will cease with the suppression of desires. The cause of frustration, which is identified as clinging or grasping, is to be found in ignorance or lack of spiritual clarity. In order to acquire spiritual clarity, we must repudiate what is generally known as "Karma," which incessantly produces the turning wheel of birth and death. This vicious circle of birth and death gives rise to "reincarnation," which will prevent us from being completely released from suffering. But, the followers of Zen Buddhism are prone to interpret this process of rebirth figuratively as a *continuing ego,* which reincarnates itself afresh at each moment of time.

The Fourth Noble Truth refers to an efficacious method to be followed for elimination of the calamitous effects of the Law of Karma. This is the Noble Eightfold Path of right belief, right aspiration, right speech, right action, right livelihood, right endeavor, right thought and right meditation. In other words we can remove all the hindrances to clarity of spiritual awareness by faithfully following the Eightfold Path referred to. Thus, we shall attain Nirvana (the blowing out of a flame) being equivalent to release or liberation in religious significance. In a word, Nirvana brings about cessation of the turnings of the Karmic wheel, while it entails the disappearance of the fruitless threshing around of the mind to grasp itself. More positively speaking, to attain Nirvana is to attain Buddhahood which allows us to transcend all dualities whatsover, such as mind and body, life and death, and right and wrong. Buddhism is the teaching of "self-enlightenment," concerning itself not with the branches and leaves, but with the root. It exhorts us to learn to listen to the voice audible within ourselves, instead of following the thoughts of other people. In this way, we can realize the oneness of all life, while the body and mind will be blended into harmonious unity.

According to Buddhism, the center of the universe lies within the subjectivity of the individual mind. Therefore, to say that God created the universe and to say simultaneously that God stands outside of the universe is tantamount to contradictory absurdity. Buddhism grasps the world as a phenomenon of flux, which consists of various spheres of relativity to the negation of the theological postulate that the world was created by some divinity, such as Almighty God.

Buddhists cannot conceive of any Savior, apart from the individual acquisition of *enlightened wisdom*. The true attitude of life which Buddhists will hold fast to is to live in this world, while freeing themselves from all mundane temptations of greediness and vain-glory. What they understand by birthlessness, unbornness, and egolessness (freedom from the vicious round of birth and death) will be attained when one lives calmly and contentedly by acting with the utmost degree of equanimity, serenity, and spontaneity. Recognition of *the voidness* transcending all forms of phenomenal objectivity is attainable only through the rejection of grasping ego. Unbornness is identical with undyingness, which will enable us to seize hold of the metaphysical meaning of timelessness. Anyone embodying this Zen spirit will never fear death. The attainment of absolute spiritual illumination will capacitate us to pay our Karmic debts once and for all, without the apprehension of our contracting new debts in the future. Unbothered by the maze of theological speculation, we shall be able to master any situation, whenever we stand in the center of the Land of Truth to be grasped subjectively.

One-pointed clear awareness reached by entering into Nirvana will induce us to focus our mind on the present. This is what might be called the gateless gate of Zen. By doing so, the past will be forgotten, while hope of the future will be willingly cancelled. So, there will be only "the Eternal Now" and this is *the suchness* of the concrete world. In the world of suchness, both *sameness* and *difference* are averred to be mere abstractions. The existential identity of the one and the many dawning upon our emancipated minds convinces us that not only man but also all other sentient and insentient beings are endowed unexceptionally with Buddhahood, whereby the dualistic view which contrasts man with nature must be cast off. As stated above, the encounter of Indian

Buddhism with Chinese Taoism has produced Zen-nism which pertains to the realm of Mahayana Buddhism. I am, however, of the opinion that Confucianism has also influenced a great deal the growth of Zen in China. In view of the fact that the origins of Zen are as much Taoist as Buddhist, it is incumbent upon us to clarify in articulate terms what is meant by Tao or the Way (Michi in Japanese). As pertinently pointed out by Dr. Alan W. Watts, there is the important difference between the concept of Tao and that of God as conceived of by the followers of Western theology. Whereas God *made* (created) the world by standing outside of it, Tao *produced* the same in the same fashion as a mother giving birth to a child. Thus, the artificial principle of "making" must be distinguished from the spontaneous principle of "growing."

The only book Lao Tze wrote is called *Tao-Te-King* and it became the basic scripture of Taoism. Let me quote some passages from the text of the *Tao-Te-King* in order to throw some light on the subtle implications of Tao, which is to be identified with Way, Truth, Reason, Orientation and Word (*Logos*). The profound meaning of the Eternal Tao is intimated as follows:

> "There is a thing inherent and natural which existed before the differentiation of heaven and earth. Motionless and unfathomable, it stands

alone and never changes. It pervades all things and never becomes exhausted. It may be designated as the Mother of the Universe. I don't know its name. But, if I am forced to give it a name, I shall call it Tao and Supreme; Supreme means going on. Going on means going far. Going far means returning."

Another passage likens the inscrutable Tao to the water:

"The weakest things in the world can overmatch the strongest things in the world. Nothing can be compared to water for its weak and yielding nature; yet in attacking the hard and the strong, nothing proves more powerful than water."

Tao is accessible only to the meek mind which practices the simple and subtle art of Wu-Wei: non-graspingness or no-mindedness. It is thanks to the constant and persevering exercise of calm meditation conducive to the realization of Wu-Wei that we shall be initiated at length into *cybernetics,* the basic pattern of self-correcting action. It is obvious that Wu-Wei propounded by Lao Tze bears a striking affinity to Nirvana in that both can deter the mind from wobbling and dithering between the alternatives or the pairs of correlative opposites, such as beauty and ugliness, and good and evil.

The *Book of Changes (I King* in Chinese) defines

Tao or the Way as the rhythmical alternation of the expansive and diversifying potency (Yin), which are perpetually at work in the universe. Besides, Tao is operative beyond the relative confines of time and space. It can be said that Tao is a permanent center of incessant mutations.

As Lao Tze asserted, all things are continuously and restlessly moving and yet each is proceeding back to its origin. Proceeding back to the origin means *quiescence*. To be in quiescence is to apprehend what amounts to *"the all-changing-changeless."* "Sudden Awakening" or Satori realized in a flash of keen insight into Buddhahood is tantamount to embodying Tao which proves identical with creative nothingness (void).

What strikes us in this connection is that Martin Heidegger, an eminent German existentialist philosopher insists on the synonymity of *Being* (Truth) and *Nothingness* as productive of a multitude of things. I guess that Heidegger's metaphysical concept of *Naught* is none other than the renewal in the Occident of Tao, upon which all things depend for existence. The Confucian doctrine of the Steadfast Mean explains likewise the alternating operation of Tao as follows:

"While there are no stirrings of pleasure, anger, sorrow, and joy, the mind may be said to be in the state of *equilibrium*. When those feelings have been stirred, and they act in their due measure, there ensues what may be called the state of *harmony*. This equilibrium is the great root from which grow all the human actions in the world, and this harmony is the universal path which one should unfailingly pursue. Let the twin principles of equilibrium and harmony prevail and a happy universal order will be brought into being throughout heaven and earth, and all things will be nourished and will flourish unobstructed."

In a word, this teaching of *matured wisdom* will acquaint us with what is usually designated as the Middle Way, to which Gautama the Buddha attached a great importance as the surest way to our deliverance from *maya*, or the labyrinth of disillusions.

In any case, Tao must be directly experienced and this esoteric method of reaching the innermost experience is described in the following verse:

"Hold fast to the All-Comprehensive Unity and concentrate your *breath* so as to make it soft like that of a little innocent child."

This description reminds us of a great deal of similarity between Taoism and the Yoga developed in India. Life pursues its course with implacableness beyond the confrontation of the beautiful and ugly.

A flower of the lotus intoxicated with her unsurpassed noble beauty happens to look at her slender stalk being submerged under the muddy water. Horrified by this nauseous sight, she tries to detach herself from the filthy mire. But, as soon as she loses contact with the sordid element, a bizarre shiver creeps stealthily over her body and her dazzlingly attractive complexion fades gradually into withering ugliness. Instinctively, she thrusts her legs again into the foul muck and only then does vital freshness come back to her benumbed and paralyzed body, to her great joy. This metaphor is an attestation of the function of vital force rising above the conflict of beauty and ugliness and spirituality and materiality.

So, any religious faith, which exalts only too one-sidedly the spiritual as detrimental to the carnal, will become self-complacently and smugly hypocritical, while it scarcely fails to provoke a vehement reaction like Marxism, which condemns the Western type of religion as an opiate likely to hypnotize the masses of the people. The Cold War waged between the two ideological quarters is traced back in the final analysis to the yawning chasm lying between religious transcendence and economic immanence.

Momozo Kurata, a great Buddhist scholar, whom I held in high esteem, once wrote from a metaphysical point of view a very illuminating essay bearing on the interconnection between peace and war. Therein he emphasized that human existence is helplessly left at the mercy of the inexorable working of *vital dialectics,* which operates ruthlessly and relentlessly beyond the dualistic opposition of war and peace and that the gross delusion, into which so-called pacifists eager to *subjectively justify themselves* are liable to fall almost unexceptionally, resides in their hesitation to candidly acknowledge the fateful correlation of peace and war, comparable to the perpetual round of birth and death. The growth of life necessitates to a considerable extent the immolation of other beings, however repulsive this dreadful claim may be to the sophisticated minds of peace mongers. It is a hypocritical absurdity to deny this objective fact in entrenching ourselves in the citadel of self-complacent subjectivism. Nevertheless, life which has grown to a certain degree of mental maturity will come to feel a strong repugnance to its sacrificing the lives of others for the sake of its survival. This is what we usually designate as Bodaishin in Japanese, which conveys somewhat the meaning of resonant *sympathy and compassion.* It is, however, tragic that, even after the awakening of this compassionate feeling, we cannot dispense with the sacrifice of other lives in order to preserve and unfold the life of our own. We are persuaded that the true connotation of the original sin will be discovered in this poignant tragedy of human existence. The flower of the lotus as a symbol of enlightened wisdom cannot blossom forth into serene splendor without sustenance of unclean mud. Yet, it is possessed of the noble mind ever anxious to achieve self-sublimation in striving to get rid of earthly impurity and defilement. Hence, it follows that the dialectical structure of cosmic vitality can reconcile the thesis of peace and the antithesis of war into what might be called "the Heavenly Decree," transcending the relative antinomy of good and evil. When we make a survey of world history in retrospect, we shall realize that stupendous modern civilization could not have been created in the West but for the slaughter of numberless living things, the utilization of slave labor, and the exploitation of the starving proletariat. This lamentable state of affairs has given rise to the fierce *struggle for existence* as conspicuously revealed in the gruesome duel of capitalism and communism carried on on a universal scale. Be that as it may, those who have shared life and destiny in strenuously endeavoring to realize social justice and communal solidarity have succeeded in establishing the humanitarian principle of *mutual assistance* capable of offsetting the evils resulting from rampancy of economic exploitism which is cognate with industrial civilization.

At the frightful sight of bloodshed, a young lady brought up in a wealthy family will be shocked much more terribly than an ignorant maid who is working in a bar room, because of the fateful concatenation of the present life and the prenatal one. Presumably, her Samurai great grandfather might have murdered in cold blood a rich merchant and appropriated to himself the fabulous fortune of the latter with impunity. He was unaware, however, that the perpetration of this heinous crime would cause his offspring to pay the Karmic debt in one way or another. It is true that his innocent descendants are not guilty in the least being unacquainted with what their forefathers have done in the past. But, they are unconsciously swayed by the irresistible urge of Karma, which links one existence inseparably to another. So, one must do his utmost to prevent the reproduction of Karma which was left over from a former existence and has heavily accumulated in the present life. The way by which complete deliverance from the Karmic Law of cause and effect is realized, is the intensification of religious life as is clearly outlined in the Eightfold Path.

The foregoing can enlighten us on the very reason why Western nations which have been pursuing imperialist policies, feel impelled to atone for their past misdeeds by championing the cause of world peace and universal brotherhood. Atrocities they have committed in regard to Asian and African people will never cease to Karmically react upon their conscientious and sensitive posterity. I believe the wholesale defeat Japan suffered will also make a large contribution to the self-exhausting of piles of Karmic retribution arising from prosecution of her pitiless

84

militarism which invited animosity and hatred of both Eastern and Western peoples.

To return to the explanation about Nirvana, this enjoyment of absolute bliss will make us understand that subjectivity and objectivity are nothing other than two grains of dust sticking to the blurred surface of a mirror. Similarly, many waves will rise and fall on the selfsame body of the expansive ocean. The image of the moon casts innumerable reflections on the water. Different ideologies like idealism, materialism, positivism, pragmatism, Marxism, and liberalism are but different facets of one and the same gem of global wisdom. Unless we put all these partialized mental actions into a bracket, so that they may be held in suspense, the true nature of Buddhahood cannot be brought to full disclosure. Then, the metaphysical import of unbornness or birthlessness (egolessness), will be thoroughly comprehended. In the light of Zen Buddhism, the many will be re-integrated into the one, just as many a climbing route converges unifyingly at the soaring summit of Mount Fuji, which commands a panoramic view over its extensive environs.

A few words must be said with regard to the conceptual differences of Tao and God. Whereas God transcendentally stands outside of the immanent world, Tao establishes balance and harmony between the spiritual and the material, having bifurcated from the oneness of ultimate reality. As Dr. Taisetsu

Suzuki says, the thinking reed (man) has been torn away from its roots, and the tremendous sweep of technological civilization is held responsible for *dehumanization,* unprecedented in its devastating effect. As a result, shallow and cheap intellectualism typified by democratism, communism, positivism and pragmatism gained wide currency among those people who are taking the lead in modern society. So the Western conventional way of thinking, which brings subject into clash with object, is incapable of coping with the situation created by the release of nuclear energy capable of destroying a great proportion of humanity.

There will be no alternative but to reach the rockbed of the "True Inner Self," analogous to the spotlessly polished surface of a mirror, for achieving complete emancipation from the modern superstition of positivistic rationalism.

Dr. Suzuki is absolutely right in stressing the urgency of abandoning our restless pursuit after power and money in order that we may plunge ourselves into the bottomless abyss of creative and all-refreshing "Nothingness" identical with a storehouse of potentialized wonders and miracles. In this regard, it is worth mentioning that Martin Heidegger strongly remonstrates against the erroneous orientation of modern Western philosophy, since it incorrigibly tends to misconstrue one of the beings *(das Seiende)* to be Being *(das Sein)* or Truth itself, thereby engendering the mess of nihilistic anarchy.

In fact, nothing will be more aberrant and mis-leading than to try rashly identifying a facet of the diamond with its total rotundity, however brilliantly it may shine forth. In the mirror of Tao, liberal democracy and Marxist communism represent but two segments of a large stone buried underground. Heidegger went so far as to claim that all the schools of Western philosophy beginning with Socrates and ending in Hegel and Nietzsche should be brought to erasure, inasmuch as they were too pre-occupied with the unilateral assertion of their narrow standpoints to be able to locate correctly and precisely where Being lurks.

I make bold to criticize the rigorously scientific method of predicting the future, because its adherents believe themselves to be able to make their decisions on the basis of relevant data which they take pains to collect as objectively as possible. But, it occurs very frequently that our plans worked out by following the positivistic method are constantly upset by entirely unforeseen events. As Dr. Alan W. Watts underscores specifically in his monumental work entitled *The Way of Zen,* the reliability of our decisions will rest ultimately upon our intuitive faculty to feel the situation. We cannot unfold such an intuitive ability otherwise than by apprehending what he calls *the peripheral vision of the mind.* This peripheral function of the mind will come into full play when we do not interfere with it rationalistically. It must be noted that this peripheral working of our psyche bringing about what might be called non-graspingness of mind seems to be closely related to the para-psychological or extrasensory perception, to which Dr. Rhine of Duke University wants to give a scientific foundation. It is only in special cases, in which the factors involved are largely mechanical or technological, that the so-called scientific method can be safely applied with no involvement of contradiction.

In refutation of the axiomatic principle of causality being strictly upheld by Western scientists, Carl Jung says that what we term *natural laws* are merely "statistical truths" allowing for some exceptions and that every process of our action is partially or totally interfered with by "chance," so much so that under natural circumstances, a course of events absolutely conforming to specific laws is almost an exception. His insistence that causality is merely a statistical truth is to be fully legitimized on account of its being in full accord with what Lao Tze propounded in his magistral treatise *Tao-Te-King*. Apropos, Judo or the Soft Way contrasting with Wrestling (the Hard Way) is virtual application of Taoist wisdom, which inculcates the lesson to yield first in order to win in the long run. Pursuant to Oriental philosophy, Tao implies not only the Way, Reason, Guidance, and Truth, but also the word (*Logos*). So, it was not accidental that the Chinese translated the first verse of the Gospel of Saint John as follows:

"In the beginning was Tao and Tao was with God and Tao was God."

The identification of Tao with God will lead to the eventual rectification of the stereotyped notion of All-mighty and All-Scient God standing outside of nature while setting transcendental spirituality at variance with immanent materiality.

As an original proponent of existentialist semantics, Heidegger posits that Being *(das Sein)* is enshrined in the bosom of the Word partaking of both physical and metaphysical natures, which are organically interwoven. Accordingly, he accentuates the importance of approaching the study of language from an existentialist point of view. He designates the language remaining unmutilated and unvitiated by the brutalizing technique of mass communication as the Domicile of Being: *die Sprache ist das Haus des Seins.* In the recesses of language, subjectivity and objectivity are meaningfully interconnected with each other. For instance, the German word "dichten" means not only to compose poetry (subjectivity), but also to thicken the quality of any liquid diluted (objectivity).

It is greatly interesting to note that this existentialist philology is strikingly akin to the Word-Soul-

Lore (Kototama no Manabi) which laid the ground-work of our ancient Shintology. For example, the word "Utsuwa" is taken to mean both a vessel and capacity, while the word "Makoto" conveys at once the meaning of sincerity (subjective) and truth (objective). Moreover, Makoto has one more connotation, the true word. So, we Neo-Shintoists bent on the achievement of a conscious resuscitation of Kototama no Manabi want to collaborate with the Western existentialists for the elaboration of a new methodology applicable to the investigation of "absolute realism," able to overcome the dichotomy of subject and object.

Many are the indications that, in the last decades, the Cosmic Pendulum has begun to shift from the trend of differentiation to that of re-integration. They are the growing interest of the Western intellectuals in "The Spiritual Technique" of Zen, universal individualism, the rapid emergence in Japan of Neo-Shintoism, the reassessment of Oriental political science designed to combine the subjective cultivation of personality (the disclosure of the hidden brilliant virtue) and the objective prosecution of statesmanship (renovation of the people), the restoration of Occidental metaphysical traditions as exemplified in existentialism, phenomenology, parapsychology, mental psychotherapy, psychosomatics and philosophical semantics, and the gradual rise of Neo-Christianity critical of the static orthodoxy of Western theology which was obviously irreconcilable with the finds of modern physical science. In this respect, what Reverend Donald Harrington of the Community Church in New York City offers as the Christian solution to a lot of vexed questions of today, deserves our particular attention on account of the profundity of his timely thought laid bare therein. He preaches among other things: the exploration of the evolutionary theory as expounded by Charles Darwin may produce the new concept of an evolutionary God to be conceived of as "Universal-Being-Becoming"; this innovating notion of God can be fully harmonized with the picture of the universe portrayed by modern science, for it is itself scientifically grounded. According to him, the evolutionary idea of God restores to man a fully responsible role, in which his daily choices are of ultimate significance. He is no longer God's puppet but a part of the God-process. This new religious conception is largely in correspondence with what the Shintoists call Shinjin Goitsu or the spiritual coalescence of Kami and Man. Reverend Harrington is far from being in agreement with the intolerant bigotry so averse to frank acceptance of scientific knowledge and method. He believes absolutely in Jesus' ethical teachings which lay claim to universality, although he rejects the Christian teaching concerning heaven and hell. As for me, I will give unconditional adherence to what was emphasized by this progressive and liberal-minded clergyman of distinction.

In addition, his fine analysis with regard to the widening fissure between self-consciousness and sub-consciousness as well as super-consciousness coupled with his postulate to vividly experience a self-transcending individuality serve to eradicate the greatest peril with which we are confronted: the incessant accumulation of power and money, as a means to maintain political hegemony, and the deplorable lack of the capacity to be spontaneously creative and original.

Note: I refer foreign students of Shinto to my work *Concrete Universality of the Japanese Way of Thinking, a New Interpretation of Shinto.*